RUNNING PRESS

DICTIONARY
OF LAW

RUNNING PRESS

DICTIONARY
OF LAW

Running Press
Philadelphia, Pennsylvania

Distributed in Canada by Van Nostrand Reinhold Ltd.,
Ontario

Edited by Peter J. Dorman

Library of Congress Cataloging in Publication Data

Running Press dictionary of law.

1. Law--United States--Dictionaries. I. Title.
II. Title: Dictionary of law.
KF156.S8   340'.03   75-40443
ISBN 0-914294-44-X lib. bdg.
ISBN 0-914294-43-1 pbk.

Art direction and interior design by Jim Wilson

Cover Lettering by Peter Ruge

This book may be ordered directly from the publisher.
Try your bookstore first.

**Running Press, 38 South Nineteenth Street,
Philadelphia, Pennsylvania 19103**

PREFACE

In its present edition, this dictionary is designed for law students, legal workers, and lay people alike. The terms contained and defined are compiled from a number of sources, including law school lectures, primary legal writings, textbooks, and casebooks. Many of the entries are not included in other law dictionaries; or, if they are included, their most common meaning is lost in a column of infrequent usages that tend to confuse and discourage even the most diligent student.

The specialized vocabulary of the law, and the increasing necessity for members of society to understand that vocabulary, dictates a general need for a convenient reference work of this type.

For the law student this dictionary is not intended to supplant the comprehensive and authoritative law dictionaries. It is meant to serve as a manageable alternative for the student's class work, and if a definition contained herein does not clarify a usage, the student would do well to note the word and check it when he or she has access to a larger work. The definitions provided here, however, should answer the needs of the beginning law student in most instances.

The reader should note that where references are made to the Code, the Internal Revenue Code is meant. The abbreviation FRCP refers to the Federal Rules and Civil Procedure, and UCC refers to the Uniform Commercial Code. Terms appearing in *italics* in the definitions are defined elsewhere in the volume.

COMMONLY USED ABBREVIATIONS AND SYMBOLS IN LAW

¶	Paragraph
§	Section (pl. §§)
Δ	Defendant
D	Defendant
π	Plaintiff
P	Plaintiff
K	Contract
C.	Chapter
SC	Supreme Court
AG	Attorney General
Ann.	Annotated

a aver et tener
To have and to hold.

ABA
American Bar Association, 1155 East Sixtieth Street, Chicago, Illinois 60637.

ABAJ
American Bar Association Journal.

abandon
To desert; to surrender; to give up rights or property.

abandonee
The party to whom something is abandoned.

ab antiquo *(Lat.)*
From ancient times.

abate
To destroy; to quash; to diminish.

abatement
A decrease; a reduction.

abduction
The crime of forcibly taking or carrying away a person. Kidnapping.

abet
To encourage; to incite.

abettor, abetter
One who abets.

abeyance
Suspension. In property, where there is no existing person in whom a property can vest, it is said to be in abeyance until a proper owner appears.

ab initio *(Lat.)*
From the beginning.

abjuration
A renunciation by oath.

abjure
To renounce; to abandon.

abode
Home; residence.

abortion
The act of bringing forth or destroying a human fetus prematurely, before it is capable of maintaining life.

abr. (abbrev.)
Abridged; abridgment.

abridge
To reduce.

abrogate
To annul; to abolish; to destroy.

abscond
To hide; to leave a jurisdiction to avoid legal process.

absolute
Complete; perfect; unconditional.

absque hoc *(Lat.)*
But for this. A phrase in pleading at common law, introducing negative averments. Compare *et non*.

abstract
To take from.

abstract of title
A condensed history of the title of a parcel of land, documenting conveyances and interests, liens, or charges on the property.

abut
To reach; to touch.

abutter
One whose property abuts or comes up against that of another.

a causa de cy
For this reason.

acceleration
The shortening of a time for the vesting of an expectant interest, performance on a contract, or payment of a note.

acceptance
In contract, consent to an offer under terms agreed to by the offeror, thereby creating a binding contract. Also, the receiving of goods with the intention of keeping them.

accession
Addition, augmentation. A right to any natural or artificial addition to one's property. E.g., gravel deposited by a river.

accessory
Anything that is joined to, incident to, or part of another greater thing; contributing to; aiding.

accomplice
One who with common intent participates with another or others in the commission or attempted commission of a crime.

accountable
Responsible; liable.

accounting period
A 12-month period for which a taxpayer's records are kept, whether a calendar year (January 1 through December 31) or a fiscal year (July 1 through June 30).

accroach
To encroach; to usurp authority.

accrual basis of accounting
An accounting basis for which income is accounted for

when earned, whether or not it is actually received.
Likewise, expenses are deducted when incurred, whether or
not they are paid during the same period. As distinguished
from *cash basis*.

accretion
The gradual and imperceptible accumulation of land,
generally by a river or a sea washing soil onto a shore.

accrue
To occur; to become due; to arise; to happen.

a contrario sensu *(Lat.)*
On the other hand.

acquiescence
Consent that is inferred from silence or from lack of express
nonconformity.

acquit
To set free; to judicially discharge from an accusation.

act in pais
A judicial act performed out of court; a judicial act not a
matter of record.

actio damni injuria *(Lat.)*
An action for damages.

actio ex delicto *(Lat.)*
An action arising from a tort.

action
A judicial remedy to enforce a right or to punish an offender;
a lawsuit.

actionable
That which might be the subject of an action.

act of God
A violent act caused by nature, without human intervention:
e.g., hurricane, tornado, earthquake.

8

actual cash value
The value at which something might be sold on an ordinary market; reasonable market price under normal circumstances.

actuary
A person who through calculations determines insurance rates and premiums.

actus reus *(Lat.)*
Criminal act. One of the elements of the *corpus delicti* of a crime.

ad *(Lat.)*
At; by; for; to.

ad curiam *(Lat.)*
To court, as in *ad curiam vocare*, to summon to court.

ad damnum *(Lat.)*
To the damage. That part of a pleading that states the plaintiff's money loss or damages claimed.

addict
A person who has formed a habit of use, especially of drugs, and who can no longer exercise self-control over that use.

additur
On appeal, in a situation in which a plaintiff is denied a new trial on the condition that the defendant agree to a specified larger settlement than that already awarded, where a court believes an award to be too low. See *remittur*.

ademption
Withdrawal or extinction of a legacy by an act of the testator. Equivalent of a revocation of a legacy.

ad gravamen *(Lat.)*
To the grievance. See *gravamen*.

adhesion contract
A contract printed as a standard form, submitted by one

party to the other on a take-it-or-leave-it basis. Adhesion contracts are commonly presented to consumers in situations where the buyer's position is substantially weaker than the seller's.

ad hoc *(Lat.)*
For special purpose, such as an *ad hoc* committee.

ad infinitum *(Lat.)*
Without limit; to infinity.

adjective law
The body of rules governing procedure or practice in legal matters, as distinguished from *substantive law*, which determines rights and duties.

adjourn
To postpone.

adjudication
A judgment.

adjunct
Additional.

ad litem *(Lat.)*
For the purposes of the suit.

administration
Management; performance.

administrative decision
A decision rendered not by a court, but by a commission established by legislation, such as the SEC or the FAA.

administrator c.t.a. *(cum testamento annexo)*
An administrator appointed to carry out the terms of a will in those cases where there is no qualified executor, whether because none was named by the testator or because the executor named is either unable or unwilling to act as administrator.

10

administrator d.b.n. *(de bonis non)*
An administrator of an estate whose duty it is to manage or distribute those parts of the estate not administered by a former executor.

admissible evidence
Evidence that may be properly received by a court considering a matter.

admission by adoption
In evidence, a declaration made in the presence of the defendant which is of such a character and is made under such circumstances as to imperatively require a denial if untrue.

ad quem *(Lat.)*
To which.

ad respondendum *(Lat.)*
For (the purpose of) answering.

ad valorem *(Lat.)*
According to value. See *tax, ad valorem*.

adversary proceeding
A trial in court where contesting parties present opposing views.

adverse possession
A means of acquiring title to real estate, through actual, notorious, exclusive and continuous occupancy of the property, under a claim of right, for a statutory period.

advisory opinion
An opinion rendered by a judge or a court, in response to a question presented by a legislative or governmental body or officer. It neither binds anybody nor decides a concrete case.

ad vitam *(Lat.)*
For life.

affiant
One who signs a written statement or an affidavit.

affidavit
A written and signed statement of fact, sworn under oath.

affirmative defense
A response to a complaint that assumes the complaint to be true but that presents a new matter as a defense. See FRCP 8(c).

affirmative easement
An easement that gives the owner of a *dominant tenement* (*q.v.*) a right of use over a *servient tenement* (*q.v.*).

affirmative relief
Relief or compensation that may be granted a defendant, apart from any claim made against him by a plaintiff.

a force
Of necessity.

a force et armis
With force and arms.

a fortiori *(Lat.)*
For a stronger reason; all the more.

agency
An arrangement or relation whereby one person represents or acts on behalf of another, with the other person's authority.

agent
A person who represents or acts on behalf of another, with the other person's implied or express permission.

aggrieved
Injured.

agreement of sale
A binding agreement between a buyer and a seller.

aid and abet
To knowingly help or encourage another to commit a crime.

aider of verdict
In a civil or a criminal case, a procedure whereby, after a verdict has been found, those facts upon which the verdict is based are presumed true and proven.

a large
Free; at large.

a latere *(Lat.)*
Collateral; from the side.

aleatory contract
An agreement in which performance by a party or parties is contingent upon an uncertain future event, such as in an insurance policy.

alias
Otherwise; an assumed name.

alien
One who is not a citizen.

alienable
That which can be transferred.

alienation
A transfer of possession of land or other things from one owner to another; the conveyance or transfer of title.

alien corporation
A corporation incorporated outside the United States or its territories. As distinguished from a *foreign corporation*, which is incorporated in another state.

aliunde *(Lat.)*
From elsewhere; from outside. Evidence aliunde may be admitted to explain an ambiguity in a will.

13   **aliquot share**   Any definite fractional interest in a trust.

allegation
Something alleged, asserted, or stated.

allege
To charge; to assert; to declare.

allocution
A formality of the court whereby it was once inquired of a defendant whether he had any legal cause why judgment should not be pronounced against him, following conviction. Today a defendant is asked whether he has anything to say in his behalf toward a mitigation of sentence.

allodial
Free; unrestricted (refers to ownership).

alluvion
The gradual increase in land by natural action of water on a shore or river bank. Distinguished from *avulsion*, which is sudden and perceptible.

alter ego *(Lat.)*
Other self. When a larger corporation controls a smaller one, a theory that allows for the dominant corporation to be held liable for negligent acts of the servient corporation.

alternative pleading
A pleading that alleges as grounds for action two contrary and mutually exclusive sets of facts. See FRCP 8(e)(2).

amanuensis
One who takes dictation or makes copies; a secretary.

ambit
A boundary line.

ambulance chaser
A lawyer who follows up on traffic accidents and encourages victims to sue. Hence, used pejoratively, any unduly aggressive lawyer.

ambulatory automatism   14

A form of automatism wherein one unconsciously wanders about, performing involuntary acts. Also, *fugues.*

amenable
Liable; responsible to answer.

amend
To change or revise, in an attempt to improve, as to *amend* a pleading.

amendment
A change; a revision.

amenity
In real estate, a feature such as view or location that renders a property pleasant and desirable for its occupants, apart from those qualities normally regarded as responsive to the occupants' needs.

amicus brief
A brief submitted by an *amicus curiae* (q.v.).

amicus curiae *(Lat.)*
A friend of the court. A qualified person or organization that provides an argument or evidence upon a matter before the court, feeling that otherwise certain relevant and important information might escape the court's attention.

amortization
The reduction of a debt by periodic payments that cover accrued interest and part of the principal.

anarchist
One who advocates a society in which there is no law or supreme authority.

ancillary
That which is subordinate to or attendant upon something else.

anent
Concerning; about; respecting; as regards.

animus *(Lat.)*
Intention.

animus furandi *(Lat.)*
Intention to steal.

animus revertendi *(Lat.)*
Intention to return (to a place).

animus revocandi *(Lat.)*
Intention to revoke.

animus testandi *(Lat.)*
Intention to make a will.

ann. (abbrev.)
Annotated.

annuitant
One who receives an annuity or regular periodic payments.

annuity
A regular periodic payment, often yearly. A fixed annual sum.

annul
To void; to nullify.

anomie
A state of mind in which the individual is without a sense of affinity with society, experiencing lack of social cohesion. The effect is that the person has no fixed values or moral standards.

anon. (abbrev.)
Anonymous.

answer
In pleading, a response to a complaint. See FRCP 7.

ante *(Lat.)*
Before.

16

ante litem motam *(Lat.)*
Before suit was brought. Before there would have been reason for anybody not to tell the truth.

ante natus *(Lat.)*
Born before. One born before another or before a special event.

anticipatory breach
In contract, a breach prior to a duty to perform, indicating an intention not to perform.

antitrust acts
Statutes to protect commerce against unlawful business trusts and monopolies.

aphasia
Loss of the ability to write or speak coherently and to understand written or spoken language; the condition results from brain damage.

a posteriori *(Lat.)*
An argument founded on fact or experimentation that proceeds to demonstrate a cause.

apparent defect
A defect in salable goods, not hidden and readily discoverable upon inspection. Contrast *latent defect*.

appeal
Application to a higher court to right an injustice or error of a lower court.

appearance
A showing-up in court, as either plaintiff or defendant in an action.

appearance, special
A submission to the jurisdiction of a court for some special purpose only, such as to contest jurisdiction or sufficiency of evidence.

appellant
One initiating an appeal to a higher court after having lost in a lower court. A petitioner.

appellate jurisdiction
Jurisdiction to review decisions of lower courts. Courts with appellate jurisdiction are generally without original jurisdiction as trial courts.

appellee
After having prevailed in a lower court, the party responding to an appeal filed in a superior court. A respondent.

apportion
To distribute proportionally.

apportionment
The division of assets, liabilities, etc., according to the respective interests of the parties involved.

appraisal
A disinterested estimation of the value of property.

appropriate
To take possession of something, particularly without permission.

appurtenance
Something annexed, attached, or belonging to some principal thing, and which passes with ownership of the principal thing — e.g., outbuildings to a farmhouse, an easement to a property. Rights and interests that are incidental.

appurtenant (to)
Belonging to.

a prendre
To take; to seize.

AR
Anno Regni. Year of the reign of a king or queen.

arbitrage
Buying and selling of stocks and bonds on two different markets, to realize a profit on the basis of a difference in price on the two markets.

arbitrament
The decision of an arbitrator.

arbitration
A method for settling controversies or disputes whereby an unofficial third party hears and considers arguments and determines an equitable settlement.

arbitration clause
A contract clause compelling parties to the contract to arbitrate differences and controversies arising from the contract.

arbitrator
An arbiter. A disinterested third party to whom a controversy is submitted for decision.

arguendo *(Lat.)*
In arguing; for the argument.

arraign
To bring a prisoner to court on an initial appearance in order to have him answer charges brought against him.

a qua *(Lat.)*
From which. The court from which a cause has been brought, whether on error, appeal, or otherwise removed, is referred to as the court *a qua*. Also, *a quo*.

arrogation
A civil law term referring to the adoption of an adult who is fully competent.

arson
Malicious burning of another's property.

asportation   Removal or carrying away of goods. Along

with a taking, a requisite of the offense of larceny.

assault
An unlawful threat to injure another person, whether by word or by deed, under circumstances calculated to produce fear and when one might reasonably expect that the threat could be carried out.

assert
To aver; to declare; to state.

assertion
A declaration; a statement.

asset
Anything of value; anything valuable that may be used to pay a debt.

assign
To convey or transfer property. To point out; to cite; to specify.

assignee
One to whom something is assigned.

assignment
An act that transfers from one person to another all or part of an interest, right, or share in property.

assignment of error
A declaration made by an appellant against a trial court, setting forth the errors complained of in such a way as to allow the *appellate court* to determine from the record the effect of the alleged errors.

assigns
Assignees.

assumpsit
At Common Law, a form of action for the recovery of a debt on a *simple contract*, or on an express or implied promise. Also, *indebitatus assumpsit*.

assythment
(In Scottish law) Damages paid by the guilty party to a relative of a murdered person, where the guilty party has not been convicted and punished.

at large
Free; not limited; without restraint. See *election at large*.

a tort
Unjustly; without reason.

attach
To take or seize property, to bring it within the custody of the court, usually to satisfy a claim.

attachment
The lawful seizure of the property of a person who is party to a suit, as security for a debt in controversy. See *garnishment*.

attainder
The termination of one's civil rights when sentenced to death, the effect of which is the forfeiture of all property.

attainder, bill of
A legislative act, passed without trial, declaring a person guilty of a capital offense. Prohibited under Article I, Section 9, of the U.S. Constitution.

attestation
Witnessing. The act of witnessing the execution of a written instrument, and subscribing, or signing it as a witness.

attractive nuisance doctrine
A doctrine assigning liability to one who maintains on his property a situation or set of circumstances under which children may be reasonably attracted to harm — e.g., an unguarded and unfenced swimming pool.

audi alteram partem *(Lat.)*
Hear the other side. No man should be condemned without being given a chance to defend himself.

automatism
A mental ailment where the person involuntarily and unknowingly commits certain acts, acts that he would presumably not have consciously committed.

autopsy
The examination of a dead body to determine the reason for the person's death.

averment
In pleading, a positive statement of facts, as opposed to an argument or a statement based on inference.

avoidability
Susceptibility to be rendered void.

avoidance
A rendering (of something) void; annulment; cancelation.

axiom
A self-evident truth; an established principle.

bail
To secure a person's liberty from legal custody by providing assurances that he will appear at a specific time and place to answer charges.

bailee
In contract, a person to whom goods are delivered.

bailiff
A steward; a keeper; a superintendent. A guardian; a sheriff's officer.

bailment
The agreement and delivery of goods in trust by one person (*bailor*) to another (*bailee*).

bailor
The person who delivers goods in trust to another.

bait and switch

A sales technique whereby a low-priced product is advertised to "bait" customers into a store to purchase, so the seller can attempt to "switch" the buyer to another product on which profits are greater.

banker's lien

A lien held by a banker, by which he can appropriate either property or money held by him, to extinguish a matured debt.

bankrupt

A person against whom a bankruptcy petition has been filed, who has filed for bankruptcy, or who has been adjudged bankrupt by the court.

bankruptcy

The condition of being bankrupt. A proceeding in which the property of a debtor person or company can be put in the control of a *receiver* or *trustee* for the benefit of creditors.

bar

To defeat; to annul; to put an end to. Something that serves as a barrier.

bargain

A contract; an agreement.

barratry

The offense of frequently instigating quarrels or suits, at law or otherwise.

barrister

In Great Britain, an attorney who tries cases. Compare *solicitor*. Loosely, in U.S. usage, any attorney.

battery

An unlawful touching, beating, or physical violence done to another without consent.

bench

The seat occupied by a judge in a court. Also, such a seat as a symbol of the office or dignity of judges as a group.

bench trial
A trial before a judge, without the benefit of a jury.

bench warrant
A warrant issued by the court for the arrest of a person in contempt or for one failing to respond to a subpoena or to appear when otherwise required. Distinguished from warrants issued by other public officers.

beneficiary
The person to whom an insurance policy is payable or for whom a trust is designated.

bequeath
To dispose of personal property by testament or will. Contrast *devise*.

bequest
Personal property given to another by will; a legacy; disposition of personal property.

best evidence
Primary or original evidence.

BIA
Bureau of Indian Affairs.

bid bond
A bond taken out as surety for a contract bid.

bigamy
The contracting of a second marriage willfully and with the knowledge that a previous marriage is yet undissolved.

bilateral
Two-sided; on both sides.

bilateral contract
A contract containing mutual promises between the parties, by which both are bound to perform. Hence, a contract in

which each party is both a promisee and a promissor.

bill
A written declaration, statement, or complaint.

billet
Military quarters. To provide quarters to military personnel.

bill of attainder
See *attainder, bill of*.

bill of exceptions
A written statement of a party's objections to rulings and instructions made by a judge during a trial.

bill of exchange
A written document, from one person to another, unconditionally ordering the receiver to pay a specific amount to a third person.

bill of lading
A written document given by a carrier of goods, describing the freight, stating the terms of the contract to carry, and agreeing that the freight should be delivered as indicated on the bill. Abbreviated B/L.

bill of particulars
Written documentation of particulars in connection with and relevant to a law suit, specifying items, dates, times, and so on, submitted either voluntarily or on court order. An account of the items of a claim. A plaintiff's informal statement of a cause of action or a defendant's set-off.

binder
In contract, a written memorandum, stating the most important items agreed upon, meant to serve as a temporary contract until a formal policy can be issued.

binding arbitration
Arbitration whose outcome is binding on both parties to the dispute.

binding instruction

An instruction to a jury by which they must arrive at a specified decision, on the basis of whether they conclude certain information to be either true or false.

bind over

A court order that an accused be held in custody pending a proceeding against him. He may then be permitted to post bond and be released.

bituminous coal

Soft coal.

black letter law

General rules of law, as derived from cases and statutes.

Blackstone, Sir William

Eminent British jurist (1723-1780); author of *Commentaries*.

blanket mortgage

A mortgage covering two or more parcels of realty.

blanket policy

In insurance, a flexible policy with broad coverage.

BLS

Bureau of Labor Statistics.

blue laws

Laws restricting commerce and labor on Sunday, often applied selectively.

blue sky laws

The popular name for laws regulating sales by investment companies, to protect investors from buying into nonexistent companies or fraudulent adventures.

BNDD

Bureau of Narcotics and Dangerous Drugs, Department of Justice.

bodily heirs   Lineal descendants.

boilerplate
In contract, sections and paragraphs of a general nature as found in a contract that do not deal with material specific to the contract.

bona fide *(Lat.)*
In good faith. Actual.

bond
A written obligation or certification of a debt.

bond, corporate
A bond, payable by a corporation to the bondholders, on a specified sum borrowed from and owed to the bondholders. The bonds are payable on a fixed date and interest is payable at a fixed rate on specified dates.

bondman, bondwoman
A person held in servitude; a slave.

bondsman
One who serves as security for another; a surety.

bottom land
Low-lying ground near a river or stream, or in a valley, which may easily flood as the result of rains or thaws.

bovines
Cattle that are either cows, calves, bulls, or steers, excluding all others. Neat cattle.

boycott
A legal or illegal attempt to coerce a position from an individual, a company, or a government, through concerted economic pressure.

Brandeis brief
A brief that discusses not so much the legal aspects of a position as opinions from other-than-judicial sources. The Brandeis brief gathers and presents information and opinions from authorities in fields germane to the argument, but without any strictly legal basis. For Louis D. Brandeis, *Muller* v. *Oregon* 208 U.S. 412 (1908).

breach of contract
Failure to perform on all or part of a contract, where there is no legal excuse for such failure.

breach of promise
A violation of a promise, ordinarily in reference to a promise of marriage.

breach of warranty
A violation of an agreement as to condition, content, or quality of a good sale, not involving fraudulent misrepresentation.

breaking bulk
An offense by a carrier in which part of the contents of a box, bale, or package in shipment are removed and converted.

breve *(Lat.; pl. brevia)*
A writ.

breve du cursu
See *writ of course*.

brief
A document prepared by counsel as a statement of the case, defining the issues, citing authorities, and presenting arguments.

brutum fulmen *(Lat.)*
An empty or harmless threat.

bulk sales acts
Statutes enacted to prevent the secret bulk sale of all or most of a business, merchandise, and stock in a business, as an effort to defraud creditors. By these statutes a business must generally list items to be sold and give creditors notice of intent to sell.

burden of proof
A requirement to prove a disputed fact.

burglary

Breaking and entering the dwelling of another in the night with intent to commit a felony, extended by statute to including breaking and entering any of various buildings by night or day.

CAB
Civil Aeronautics Board.

cabal
A small group of associates, organized to intrigue. An intrigue.

calumny
Slander; false accusation of a crime.

camera stellata *(Lat.)*
See *Star Chamber*.

canon
A law or rule, particularly of the church under ecclesiastical law.

capias ad satisfaciendum *(Lat.)*
That you take to satisfy. A writ for the arrest and detention of a person against whom judgment for the payment of a sum of money has been rendered, until such time as payment is made.

capital assets
All assets except those held for sale to customers in the ordinary course of the taxpayer's trade or business. For exceptions, see Code Sec. 1221.

capital gains
Gains realized from sale or exchange of capital assets. See

capital losses
Losses realized from sale of capital assets. See Code Sec. 1222.

29   **capital punishment**   Punishment by death.

capital stock
The face value of the combined interest of all the corporation stock of a corporation's stockholders.

capitation tax
A tax levied on a person, regardless of his ability to pay. A poll tax.

caption
The felonious taking of goods (with *asportation* (q.v.), the carrying away), as an aspect of larceny.

cartel
An association of producers, to regulate output, sale, and price of a commodity or indusltry, to obtain a monopoly.

ca. sa. *(Lat.,* abbrev.*)*
Capias ad satisfaciendum (q.v.).

case
An action or a question contested in a court of law or equity. A short form of *trespass on the case*.

case law
A body of jurisprudence emanating from adjudged cases and concrete facts, as opposed to that emanating from statutes or constitutions, which arises from abstract principles.

case or controversy
A phrase referring to a bona fide dispute that may be decided by a court of justice.

cash basis of accounting
An accounting basis for which income is accounted for only as received and expenses are deductible only for the year during which they are paid. As distinguished from *accrual basis*.

cash market value
Fair market value.

casual employment
Employment on an irregular or uncertain basis. Sporadic; by chance; for temporary purpose.

casuistry
A generally disparaging reference to techniques of false reasoning in determining right from wrong.

causa *(Lat.)*
Cause; reason.

causa mortis *(Lat.)*
Because of death. In contemplation of death. A *donatio causa mortis* is a gift of personal property made as one is about to die, and does not take effect unless the donor actually dies.

causa proxima *(Lat.)*
Proximate or nearest cause.

caveat *(Lat.)*
Let him beware. A warning or caution.

caveat emptor *(Lat.)*
Let the buyer beware. Indicating that the buyer is responsible for the worth and worthiness of goods purchased.

caveat venditor *(Lat.)*
Let the seller beware. Indicating that the seller is responsible for deficiencies in goods sold.

cede
To yield; to assign.

certiorari
A discretionary writ in an appellate proceeding, to review questions of law or procedure in the interest of justice.

cestui que trust
A person who has a right or interest in an estate, where legal title is vested in another. A *trustee*.

cestui que vie
The person whose life is the measure of a life estate.

C&F
Cost and Freight.

cf. *(Lat.* abbrev. *confer)*
Compare.

challenge for cause
A challenge of a prospective juror for some reason, as opposed to a *peremptory challenge (q.v.)*.

chamberlain
An officer whose duties are those of a treasurer.

champerty
An agreement between a party to a suit and a disinterested party, by which the latter will carry on litigation on behalf of the former and against another party in consideration for a part or percentage of the proceeds if successful.

chancery
A court of equity. *Equity.*

charge
An accusation. To accuse. To instruct a jury. To claim.

charitable institution
A nonprofit institution maintained by charity or by public funds, usually for the benefit of a specific class of persons.

chattel
Movable or personal property, including both animate and inanimate property.

chattel mortgage
A *mortgage* on tangible person property.

chimera
A fanciful and impossible creation of the imagination.

chimerical
Imaginary; unreal; impossible.

chiromancy
Fortune-telling by studying the palm of the hand. Palmistry.

choate lien
A definite enforceable lien, in which both the lienor and the subject property are established.

choice-of-law
In conflict of laws, when a court must choose between its laws and the laws of a foreign jurisdiction.

chose in action
A debt, damages, or property wrongfully held by another and recoverable by lawsuit.

cite
To summon. To refer to.

civil action
Any action that is not a criminal action.

civil law
Law that developed under the Roman Empire and that has survived in all the European countries except Great Birtain. Civil law is based on codes rather than on custom, and is distinguished from the common law. Also, Roman law.

claimant
A person who claims or asserts a right or who voluntarily applies for justice.

class action
A lawsuit brought by one or more persons on behalf of a class of persons similarly situated, usually where the number of persons in the class is too great for all to appear in court. See FRCP 23.

clean hands
A principle that may be asserted to prevent equitable relief

from being granted to one who himself has acted unjustly or unfairly in the transaction giving rise to the action.

clear title
Good, marketable title; title free from encumbrances.

close
A parcel of land enclosed by a hedge or fence.

close corporation
A corporation in which the majority of the stock is held by the officers and directors. E.g., a corporation owned and operated primarily by a single family.

closed shop
A shop or business establishment where a worker must be a union member as a condition of employment; illegal under the National Labor Relations Act.

cloture
In parliamentary procedure, the means by which debate is ended and a vote taken.

cloud on title
An invalid claim on a title, but one that on its face appears valid and that, if true, would affect the title.

COD
Collect (cash) on delivery.

codicil
A written revision or addendum to a prior will, executed with the same formalities as a will.

cognizable
Within the jurisdiction of the court or other tribunal.

cognovit
A defendant's written acknowledgment of guilt under a complaint, as authority for entry of judgment against him.

34

collateral
Additional; supplementary; complementary. Property subject to a security interest.

collateral attack
A proceeding that is separate and remotely incidental to an issue, but that is brought to void a previous valid judgment on that issue.

collateral estoppel
An estoppel resulting from a previous collateral decision on the same issue and between the same litigants, by a court of competent jurisdiction. Issue preclusion.

collude
To conspire for fraudulent purposes.

collusion
The secret agreement between two presumably hostile parties to act to the detriment of a third party, or for some other improper purpose.

collusive action
An action brought by two parties not actually adversaries and for whatever purpose, although they purport to be bona fide litigants. Courts do not entertain such actions.

color
A deceptive appearance that, being one thing, represents another.

colorable
That which can be made to appear valid, but which is not. Deceptive.

color of law
The appearance of legal right, where in fact there is none.

comity
Courtesy; respect. See *judicial comity*.

Commerce Clause

Article I, Section 8, Clause 3, U.S. Constitution: "The Congress shall have the power . . . (3) to regulate commerce with foreign nations, and among the several States . . ."

commingle

To mix together; to combine in a single mass.

commit

By lawful authority, to send a person to prison, to a reformatory, or to an asylum.

commodities

Articles or goods of trade or commerce.

commodum ex injuria sua nemo habere debet
(Lat.)

No person should derive benefit from his own wrong.

common carrier

A person or company in the business of transporting passengers or goods for profit.

common law

That body of law and legal theory that is based on customs and usages that originated and developed in England. As distinguished from the Roman law, modern civil law, canon law, and other legal systems.

common law crime

A crime that could be punished under the common law, as distinguished from crimes punishable under statutes.

common stock

Corporation stock representing an interest that is subordinate to other interests in the corporation, such as bonds and preferred stock, etc. Holders of common stock have an advantage over bondholders and preferred stockholders in that common stockholders are permitted to vote for directors, whereas preferred stockholders generally are not permitted to participate in corporation management.

commutation
A change. In criminal law, following conviction and sentencing of the defendant, a reduction in sentence.

commute
To reduce the sentence of one convicted of a crime.

comp. (abbrev.)
Compiled; compilation.

competent
Qualified; meeting all requirements; of sufficient mental capacity as required by law.

competent court
A court having lawful jurisdiction.

complainant
One who seeks legal remedy in the courts; a *plaintiff*.

compound a felony
To agree for valuable consideration not to prosecute a felony. To agree with a felon not to prosecute a crime committed against one's person or property, in exchange for reparations.

comptroller
A public or private employee responsible for fiscal affairs, whose duty it is to oversee expenditures, to maintain records, and to report on the financial situation from time to time. Also, controller.

compulsory nonsuit
See *involuntary nonsuit*.

compurgation
See *wager of law*.

compurgator
See *wager of law*.

concealment
Fraudulent hiding or withholding of information or evidence that one is bound to reveal.

conclusion of fact
An inference made from facts in evidence.

conclusion of law
A conclusion drawn from rules of law, as applied to specific facts as pleaded.

concur
To agree.

concurrent
At the same time; contemporaneous; running together.

concurrent jurisdiction
See *coordinate jurisdiction*.

condemnation
The taking of private property for public use, without the owner's consent but upon payment of just compensation.

conditional sale
A sale on credit, wherein title to the goods sold does not pass until the full price has been paid. The seller thereby retains the right to repossess, and often may be able to accelerate payments if the buyer fails to meet the terms of the contract, e.g., by falling behind on payments.

condominium
Ownership in fee of a specific area in a multiple dwelling — an apartment in an apartment building — with tenancy in common ownership of the common areas, such as corridors, parking lots, etc.

confession and avoidance
At common law, a plea that confessed the allegations made against a party, and that then alleged new matter that rendered the charges legally void (avoided).

confession of judgment
A written promise by a debtor that acknowledges the jurisdiction of a court and that upon default allows judgment to be entered against him, without requiring formal action on the part of the creditor. A confession of judgment might be included as a contract clause.

conflict of laws
That contradicition or inconsistency in laws of different jurisdictions, relating to a subject matter of an action brought in one of the jurisdictions, where a party to the action or the subject matter is from the other jurisdiction.

confusion
A merger; an intermingling.

confute
To prove a statement or an argument to be wrong, false, or invalid.

conglomerate
A number of corporations engaged in unrelated business activities that are controlled by a single large corporation.

conjugal
Of, belonging to, or arising from the husband-wife relationship.

consanguinity
Relationship by blood, although not necessarily in the same generation.

consent
Voluntary compliance; agreement.

consent judgment
An agreement by the parties to an action, entered into with the approval of the court and acknowledged and recorded by the court. A settlement agreed to by the parties to an action.

consideration
The price or motive for inducement of a contract, without which a contract is not binding (with a few exceptions). Consideration may be in the form of a prejudice suffered, a benefit conferred, an obligation accepted, or other tangibles or intangibles.

consideration, good
See *good consideration*.

consideration, legal
See *legal consideration*.

consideration, valuable
See *valuable consideration*.

consign
To leave in the custody of a middleman. To deliver in trust to a third person goods or valuables intended for a principal to an agreement.

consortium
Companionship of a spouse, resulting from the marital relationship, the purposeful interference of which is actionable in tort.

conspiracy
An unlawful agreement between two or more parties to act to the harm or detriment of another party or other parties.

constitution
The basic, fundamental, organic law of a state or nation.

construction
The determination of the sense or meaning or the interpretation of a law or statute, as it applies to a specific set of facts.

constructive
Implied by law, although not actually apparent by fact; inferred.

40

constructive eviction
Eviction by breach of covenants by a landlord; an impairment of a tenant's quiet enjoyment of premises, legally amounting to an intent to oust.

constructive trust
A trust by operation of law, as distinguished from an express trust. By construction of law, a court will establish a constructive trust in favor of one party and against another, when title is actually in the name of the latter, but when by either mistake or fraud the former has been deprived of what is rightfully his.

construe
To arrive at a meaning of the language of a statute, contract, or statement, by inference or construction.

contemner
One guilty of *contempt*.

contempt
Willful disregard or disobedience of authority, whether judicial or legislative.

contiguous
In close proximity, although not necessarily in contact.

contingent
Potential or possible, although uncertain; where there is no present interest.

contingent claim
A claim dependent upon a future event that may or may not transpire.

contingent fee
A lawyer's fee for services, to be paid only in the event of success.

contingent remainder
See *remainder*.

41   **continuance** Postponement of an action pending in court.

contra *(Lat.)*
Against; opposite.

contraband
Goods imported, exported, or held, in violation of law; prohibited goods.

Contract Clause
Article I, Section 10, Clause 1, U.S. Constitution: "No State shall . . . pass any . . . law impairing the obligation of contracts . . ."

contra proferentem
Against the party putting it forward.

contributory negligence
Negligence on the part of the plaintiff, adding to or compounding the plaintiff's injury and sometimes barring recovery.

controversy
A justiciable dispute; a dispute between legal interests of adverse parties.

controvert
To contest; to dispute; to deny.

contumacy
Refusal of a party before the court to obey the court's demands; refusal to appear in court to answer charges. Primarily ecclesiastical law.

conversion
Unauthorized and wrongful assumption of ownership of goods known to belong to another.

convey
To transfer title or ownership of property.

conveyance
A transfer of title to real estate; the instrument transferring such title.

coparcener
One holding land by *coparceny*.

coparceny
A tenancy existing where real property descends by inheritance to two or more females only. Coparceners hold as tenants in common, with no right of survivorship (see *survivorship, right of*).

coordinate jurisdiction
Jurisdiction by equally competent courts, over the same parties and subject matter, at the same time.

copyright
A property right in authors, providing them exclusive privilege over their literary works for a period of time established by Congress under Article I, Section 8, Clause 8, of the U.S. Constitution, which states: "The Congress shall have the power (8) To promote the progress of science and the useful arts, by securing for limited times to authors . . . the exclusive right to their . . . writings. . . ."

coram *(Lat.)*
In the presence of.

coram ipso rege *(Lat.)*
In the presence of the king himself.

coram nobis *(Lat.)*
In our presence. A writ of coram nobis. In calling the court's attention to errors of fact that would constitute a valid defense, when those errors were not brought out in a previous trial resulting in a conviction, and when they would presumably have prevented the judgment. A writ of coram nobis may raise later-discovered issues of evidence, and serves to attack a conviction not currently being served.

coram non judice *(Lat.)*
In the presence of a court of incompetent jurisdiction, and hence void.

coram vobis *(Lat.)*
In your presence; as in a writ of error directed to the court that tried the matter.

coroner
A county official whose duty it is to inquire into the manner and cause of deaths in his territory in cases where there is suspicion of foul play.

corporeal hereditaments
Tangibles that may be inherited, such as lands, buildings, vehicles, and the like.

corpus delicti *(Lat.)*
The body of the offense; i.e., proof that a crime has been committed.

corroborate
To support credibility; to reinforce.

cost-plus contract
A contract that establishes the amount to be paid to the contractor as the price of labor and materials, plus a specified percentage of that price.

cotenancy
A broad term referring to joint ownership, involving the *unity of possession*.

cotenant
One holding property by *cotenancy*.

count
Each part of a criminal indictment, charging a separate indictable offense.

counterclaim
A claim by a defendant in response to a complaint, to deduct from or to defeat the complaint. See FRCP 8, 13, and 28.

countersign
To sign a document to confirm the authenticity of a previous

signature by another party.

court of common pleas
In some states, a court of original and general jurisdiction.

court of last resort
A court from which there is no appeal.

court martial
A military court for trying offenses against the military by members of the military.

coutume
Custom. In French, the nearest equivalent for the English "common law."

covenant
An agreement written into a deed or other document, promising performance or nonperformance of certain acts, or fixing certain uses or nonuses for the property.

covenantee
One to whom a covenant is made.

covenantor
One making a covenant.

covenant, restrictive
A covenant restricing either land use or alienation.

coverture
The state of a woman while married. Coverture has traditionally had implications regarding a woman's rights, such as rendering a woman legally incompetent.

CPI
Consumer Price Index.

creditor
One to whom a debt is owed.

crimen falsi
Falsehood and fraud in impeding the administration of justice. A general classification of offenses involving deceit, such as forgery, fraudulent alteration of a document, or perjury.

criminal action
A proceeding in which a person who is charged with a criminal offense is brought to trial, tried, and judged.

criminal conversation
Adultery, constituting a civil injury.

cross-claim
The claim by a party to a lawsuit against a coparty, arising out of the transaction or occurrence that is the subject matter of the original action or of a counterclaim in the original action, or relating to property that is the subject matter of the original action. See FRCP 13(g).

cross-complaint
See *counterclaim*.

cross examination
The questioning of a witness by a party other than the one calling the witness to the stand; questioning by the adverse party.

culpable
Blamable.

cum onere *(Lat.)*
With burden. Something taken *cum onere* is accepted with any existing *encumbrances*.

curtesy
The common law estate allowing a husband to a life estate in his wife's fee simple or fee tail estates after her death.

custodia legis *(Lat.)*
In custody of the law. Refers to property taken by virtue of legal process.

46

cy pres
So near. A rule of construction for wills, in which the original intent of the testator is either impossible or illegal. The court will construe the closest legal meaning possible, so as to give some effect to the testator's intent.

damage feasand (damage faisant)
Doing damage. The act of animals' entering property, feeding upon, and tramping down growing crops.

damages
Monetary compensation, or remuneration, allowed by the courts for a person sustaining injury through the unlawful acts of another.

damages, actual
Damages paid that amount to the actual loss sustained.

damages, exemplary
Punitive damages. In a tort action, damages paid to a plaintiff in excess of his actual loss, to serve as punishment for vicious, fraudulent, or otherwise evil behavior on the part of the defendant.

damages, liquidated
The amount established by the parties to a contract that must be paid by one or either of the parties in the event of a default or breach.

damages, special
Damages arising directly from a set of circumstances, although not necessarily following from them.

damnatus *(Lat.)*
Prohibited by law.

damnum *(Lat.)*
Damage.

damnum absque injuria *(Lat.)*
Damage or loss for which there is no legal remedy; hence it cannot give rise to an action for damages.

dangerous per se
A thing dangerous in itself, which may cause harm without human intervention — e.g., dynamite.

dans et retiens nihil dat *(Lat.)*
He who gives and retains, gives nothing.

d.b.a.
Doing business as. Indicates an unincorporated business affiliation of an individual. E.g., John Doe d.b.a. Ajax Appliance Repair.

D.C.
District of Columbia. District Court.

debase
To lower in character, rank, estimation, or value.

de bene esse *(Lat.)*
Conditionally. With reference to appearance of a witness or presentation of evidence, the court may accept depositions or evidence *de bene esse*, i.e., on the condition and assumption that the deponent, etc., may not be available at a later date. Abbreviated *d.b.e.*

debenture
An unsecured bond; a corporate or public company bond that contains a promise by the corporation to pay its debt to the bondholder, although the promise is not supported by security. A certificate acknowledging a debt.

debit
A sum owed and due; an amount set down as a debt. A bookkeeper's term, to refer to the left page of a ledger.

debt
Something owed by one person to another, whether goods, money, or services, as a bill bond or note, or by other agreement or contract.

debtee
One to whom a debt is owed.

48

debtor
One owing a debt.

decapitation
Beheading.

decedent
A deceased person.

declaratory judgment
A decision by a court, outlining the rights and duties of parties to a dispute, but without coercing any performance with respect to those rights.

decree
A judgment or order issued by a court.

decree nisi
A court's provisional decree, to become final at a specified later time unless the person against whom it is given shows good cause why it should not become final.

de die in diem *(Lat.)*
From day to day.

de donis conditionalibus *(Lat.)*
Concerning conditional gifts. An English statute passed in 1285, by which the estate in fee tail was created, introducing perpetuities and strengthening the power of the barons by allowing their estates to build up.

deed
A conveyance of a present interest in real estate.

de facto *(Lat.)*
Actually; in fact. Often contrasted with *de jure*, which means rightful or legitimate.

defalcation
Defaulting. A failure to account for funds; not necessarily implying fraud or other dishonesty.

defamation
Injury to one's reputation.

default
An omission or a failure to perform a duty that one is legally bound to perform. A failure to take the required steps in a court action.

defeasible
Subject to being divested or revoked upon the happening of some contingency.

defeasible fee
A fee that may be defeated upon the happening of some contingency, i.e., subject to defeat if certain conditions are not met.

defeat
To prevent; to terminate; to undo.

defect
An imperfection; a flaw. The want or lack of something required by law.

defendant
In a court action, the person defending; the one against whom an action is brought.

defendant in error
A party in whose favor a judgment was rendered, which judgment the losing party seeks to have reversed or revised in a higher court on a writ of error.

deferred payments
Installment payments.

deficiency judgment
An action of foreclosure on a mortgage.

definitive
Absolute; final; complete.

deforce
To wrongfully withhold from the rightful possessor possession of real property.

dehors *(Fr.)*
Beyond; outside of. E.g., *dehors*, or not contained within, the record.

Dei gratia *(Lat.)*
By the grace of God.

de jure *(Lat.)*
By law; rightful; legitimate. Often contrasted with *de facto*, which means actually, or in fact.

deleterious
Harmful; injurious.

delictum *(Lat.)*
A crime; a tort; a wrong in general.

dem. (abbrev.)
Demise.

demand note
A note expressly stating that something is payable on demand.

de minimus non curat lex *(Lat.)*
The law does not concern itself with trivial matters.

de minis
A writ of threats, where a person was threatened with bodily harm or destruction of property, to compel the offender to desist.

demise
A transfer or conveyance, either in fee, for life, or for years. A lease for a term of years.

demur
To object formally to a pleading.

demurrant
One who demurs.

demurrer
A motion to dismiss for failure to state a claim. See FRCP 12(b).

de novo *(Lat.)*
Once again. A writ *venire de novo* serves to summon a jury for a second trial on a case remanded for a new trial, in keeping with instructions from a higher court.

deplete
To reduce in quantity; to lessen; to exhaust.

dépeçage *(Fr.)*
In conflict of laws, when a case presents more than one issue, the application of the laws of different jurisdictions to determine the different issues.

deponent
One who testifies under oath; one who deposes.

depose
To testify under oath. To unseat a person from public office.

deposition
A written record of sworn testimony, made before a public officer for purposes of a court action, usually in the form of answers to questions posed by a lawyer. Depositions are used for the discovery of information or as evidence at a trial.

derivative
From another; owing its existence to something previous.

derivative action
A suit brought by a shareholder on behalf of a corporation and against a third party.

derogate
To impair; to partially repeal; to reduce in effect.

desuetude
Disuse.

detainer
The holding of a person's goods against his will; detention.

deter
To discourage; to stop.

determinable
Liable to terminate on the happening of some contingency.

determinative
That which determines; conclusive; determining.

devest
See *divest*.

devise
Disposition of real property by will, or an instrument directing such disposition. Note: a dispostion of personal property is a *bequest* (*q.v.*).

devisible
That which can be devised.

devolve
To fall upon; to pass from one person to another.

dicta *(Lat.,* pl. of *dictum,* for *obiter dictum)*
Something said in passing. Words in a written opinion not necessary to the decision, but as general comment of the judge in considering the case.

dilatory
Tending or intended to delay.

dilatory defense
A defense that does not go to the merits of the case, but rather attempts to delay the action until the obstacle — e.g., challenge of jurisdiction, disability of one of the parties — insisted upon is removed.

diminution
A decrease; a reduction.

dipsomania
An uncontrollable impulse to become intoxicated.

directed verdict
A verdict rendered by the jury, at the direction of the court, where evidence is insufficient, where the overwhelming weight of the evidence is for one party, or where the law as applied to the facts demands such a verdict.

direct examination
The initial interrogation of a witness by the person calling him to the stand.

direct tax
A tax imposed directly on real property. Forbidden by Article I, Section 9, Para. 4, of the U.S. Constitution, but later permitted under the 16th Amendment.

disaffirm
To repudiate.

disciplinary rules
From the Code of Professional Responsibility of the American Bar Association, the particular canons that, if violated, will subject the violator to sanctions, as applicable to members of the legal profession.

disclaimer
A disavowal or repudiation of right, interest, or responsibility.

disclosure
Revelation.

discovery
A method whereby opposing parties in a proceeding may obtain information from one another through interrogatories, depositions, inspection of pertinent documents, etc., to establish the points of dispute prior to

going to trial. Either party may compel disclosure of relevant material. See FRCP 26-37.

discrete
Separate; individual; not part of a corpus.

disinter
To exhume; to take out of the grave.

disjunctive allegation
A pleading in the alternative of two mutually exclusive charges connected with the conjunction "or."

dismissal without prejudice
Dismissal of an action specifically not barring subsequent action on the same cause.

dismissal with prejudice
A final disposition of an action, with a bar to a right to bring any other action on the same cause.

disposition
A willingness. Also, the way in which a case is ultimately disposed of, i.e., the outcome.

dispossess
To eject; to legally oust from land.

disseisin
The dispossession, or the wrongful putting out, of the rightful possessor of a freehold. A deprivation of possession.

dissemble
To conceal or disguise real appearance and to feign otherwise.

dissentiente (Lat.)
Dissenting.

dissolute
Lewd; profligate; wanton.

dissent — disagree

distrain
To seize goods or chattels by distress.

distraint
Seizure of property. Where a person liable for a debt neglects or refuses to make payment, his personal property may be distrained, or taken over, and either held until the debt is satisfied or sold in satisfaction of the debt.

distress
To take without legal process goods and chattels of a wrongdoer, to procure payment, e.g., of rent or of damages caused.

diversity of citizenship
In reference to jurisdiction in the federal courts, the situation that obtains when parties to a lawsuit are from different states. Where diversity of citizenship is the basis for federal jurisdiction, all of the parties on one side of the controversy must have diversity of citizenship from all of the parties on the other side of the controversy. If there is any common citizenship of adverse parties, diversity is defeated. See the U.S. Constitution, Article III, Section 2, and the 11th Amendment.

divest (devest)
To take away: to deprive a person of some authority, property, right, or title.

dividends exclusion
Every private taxpayer may exclude from his gross income the first $100 of dividends received in the year. Note that dividends from some insurance companies, foreign corporations, and other sources do not qualify for this exclusion.

DJ
District Judge.

docket
A calendar or agenda of court proceedings, as prepared by the clerk of the court.

doctrine of presumed grant
A doctrine allowing for a fictitious grant that is established by the presumption of a title by prescription, used to quiet title to land held by adverse possession.

doing business
A corporation's conduct or management of business within a jurisdiction, as a continuous and systematic effort, so as to render the corporation subject to the jurisdiction of the local courts.

domesday book
A record book made in the years 1085–1087, in which were recorded most of the holdings in England and that served as documentation for deeds where they were otherwise unwritten.

domestic corporation
A corporation incorporated under the laws of a state, as opposed to a *foreign corporation*.

domicile
A person's permanent residence; the place to which a person intends to return, whenever away, and where he intends to remain for any length of time.

domiciliary
Relating to one's *domicile*.

dominant tenement
The estate for which an easement exists, as against the *servient tenement*.

domitae naturae *(Lat.)*
Domestic animals. Animals that are generally tame and only in exceptional cases wander at large. Opposite of *ferae naturae*.

donatio causa mortis
See *causa mortis*.

57   **donatio inter vivos** *(Lat.)* A gift between living persons

dower
A common law estate in a wife to one third of the lands held in fee simple or fee tail by the husband during their marriage.

dowry
The property a woman brings to her husband in marriage.

Draco
From 7th Century B.C. Greece, the semi-mythical propounder of a set of severe criminal laws.

draconian
With reference to a set of severe criminal laws purported to be by Draco, 7th Century B.C. Greece. Hence, unduly severe.

drayage
The transportation of goods.

drayman
One engaged in the transportation of goods.

dubitante *(Lat.)*
Doubting. Affixed to a judge's name in court reports, indicating that he doubts the correctness of the decision.

duces tecum, subpoena
Bring with you. A subpoena requiring the person summoned to take to court certain specified documents or evidence, to be submitted in court. See *subpoena*.

dum fervet opus *(Lat.)*
While the work glows. In the heat of action.

dun
To urge or demand payment.

duress
Coercion; threats.

Durham Rule
A test for criminal responsibility, based on irresistible

58

impulse. If it is beyond a reasonable doubt that a defendant was of diseased and defective mental capacity when he committed a crime, and that the crime was the product of the mental state of the defendant, the Durham Rule maintains that he cannot be held criminally responsible for his acts.

DWI
Died without issue; childless.

earnest money
An amount paid by a buyer in order to bind a seller to the terms of an agreement; a deposit.

easement
A nonpossessory right or privilege held by the owner of an estate (the dominant tenement) concerning another estate (the servient tenement) for some special purpose, while the owner of the latter may not interfere with the owner of the former in the exercise of the right or privilege. An easement is classified as an incorporeal hereditament.

easement, affirmative
An easement that allows for some action to be performed on the premises of the servient tenement — e.g., a right of way.

easement, appurtenant
An easement concerning the property that passes automatically with title from one owner to another.

easement in gross
A personal easement, not appurtenant to an estate and not transferable.

ed. (abbrev.)
Editor; edition.

EEO
Equal Employment Opportunity.

EEOC
Equal Employment Opportunity Commission.

e.g. *(Lat.* abbrev.*)*
Exempli gratia. For example.

egregious
Negatively exceptional. Remarkable for negative qualities.

ejectment
An action to regain possession of premises, as well as to win damages for unlawful retention. Not applicable in landlord-tenant situation.

ejusdem generis *(Lat.)*
Of the same kind or class.

election at large
An election by direct vote of the people.

eleemosynary
Charitable.

emancipate
To set free.

embezzlement
The fraudulent appropriation to one's own use of money or goods entrusted to one's care by another.

emblements
Crops planted annually on a property, by labor and industry (not including orchard crops). Fructus industriales.

embolism
The obstruction of a blood vessel by a body traveling in the blood — e.g., a blood clot, an air bubble.

embracery
Attempted corruption of a juror, by threats, promises, etc. Jury fixing.

eminent domain
A right in the government to take property for public use, upon payment of just compensation. Eminent domain is

asserted for construction of public highways, public buildings, and the like.

emolument
Profits arising from one's employment or office, whether in the form of salary, advantages, fees, or other gain.

empanel (impanel)
To select jury members.

emplead
To accuse; to bring a charge.

emptor *(Lat.)*
A buyer; a purchaser.

enable
To give authority or power to do something.

en banc
On the bench. With all of the judges of the court sitting.

enceinte *(Fr.)*
Pregnant.

encroach
To intrude gradually. To advance beyond proper and prescribed limits.

encumbrance
A claim or lien against property. Also, *incumbrance.*

endorse
The writing of a name on the back of a document, such as a check, whereby the property in the name written is assigned to another. Also, *indorse.*

en gros
In gross. Wholesale.

enjoin
To command or require. On a court order, to require a person to do or to keep from doing something.

entrapment
An act by a law enforcement officer to induce a person to commit a crime that the person had not previously contemplated.

entrust
To deliver something to another in trust, with a mutual understanding as to what use is to be made of it and with the belief that the understanding will be honored. Also, *intrust*.

entry, writ of
A writ to recover real property wrongfully withheld.

enure
To take effect. To serve to a person's use or advantage. Also, *inure*.

EO
Executive Order.

eo nomine *(Lat.)*
Under that name.

EPA
Environmental Protection Agency.

e pluribus unum *(Lat.)*
Out of many, one. The motto of the United States of America.

equitable
Just; fair.

equitable conversion
A court's constructive exchange of property from real to personal property, or vice versa, to give effect to stipulations of a contract or to directions in a will, even though no such exchange has actually occurred.

equity
Fairness. Moral justness. The interest held by a property owner over and above mortgage indebtedness on the property.

escalator clause
Ordinarily, when rent or price control is involved, a contract clause that allows for rent or price to be raised in accordance with rises in costs or expenses, because of inflation, shortages, etc.

escheat
Transfer of property to the state because of abandonment or lack of an owner, often in the event of a death intestate where there are no ascertainable heirs.

Escobedo Rule
When an investigation begins to focus on a particular suspect, and the police take the suspect into custody to elicit incriminating testimony, the suspect must be warned of his right to remain silent and to consult with an attorney. If these provisions are not met, the Escobedo Rule maintains that no statement made by the suspect while being interrogated may be used against him in a criminal action. Escobedo v. Illinois, 378, U.S. 478 (1964).

escrow
The delivery of a document to a third party, in trust, to be delivered to the benefited party upon satisfaction or performance of certain specified conditions.

Establishment Clause
The First Amendment guarantee that "Congress shall make no law respecting an establishment of religion. . . ."

estate by the entireties
A common law estate that holds that an estate in a husband and wife is but one estate, a joint-tenancy with right of survivorship.

estate for years
An estate that terminates after a specified period of time,

stated in advance, whether for a year or years, or only months or weeks.

estate in severalty
An estate held by a single person, with no other person holding a concurrent interest.

estop
To bar; to preclude; to prevent.

estoppel
A bar. A statement or admission that prevents the person making it from producing evidence to controvert it. Such a declaration would be of such a substantial nature that it would allow for no dispute by the person making it.

estovers
The right to use wood from leased premises for purposes of maintaining the premises — e.g., for fenceposts, repairs to buildings, and so on.

et al. *(Lat.* abbrev.*)*
Et alii. And others (or *et alius,* and another).

ethical consideration
From the Code of Professional Responsibility of the American Bar Association, a statement of a general desirable level of conduct on the part of members of the legal profession.

etiology
The science of causes or origins.

et non *(Lat.)*
And not. A phrase in pleading, introducing negative averments. Compare *absque hoc.*

et ux. *(Lat.* abbrev.*)*
Et uxor. And wife.

euthanasia
The act of painlessly putting to death a person suffering from

a painful and incurable disease.

eviction
Lawful entry and dispossession of real property.

ex aequitate *(Lat.)*
From or in equity.

except
To take *exception* (q.v.); to exclude; not including.

exceptant
One taking an *exception* during a proceeding.

exception
During a trial, an objection to a court action or ruling. The party taking the exception notes for the record that he does not accept the court's action, and will attempt to reverse its consequences at a later opportunity, should it become necessary.

exchequer
In England, the department of government corresponding to the U.S. Department of the Treasury.

exclusive agency to sell
Exclusive right to sell a manufacturer's product or a parcel of land.

exclusive jurisdiction
A court's jurisdiction over a proceeding, at the exclusion of all other courts.

ex colore officii *(Lat.)*
By color of office. An erroneous assumption of a right to perform some act by authority of one's office.

ex contractu *(Lat.)*
From a contract. One of the two sources of obligations and causes of action, the other being *ex delicto* (q.v.).

exculpatory
Excusing; diminishing or extinguishing blame.

ex delicto *(Lat.)*
From a tort. One of the two sources of obligations and causes of action, the other being ex *contractu* (q.v.).

execute
To perform; to make or do. Performance of all necessary formalities, including signing and delivering.

execution sale
A sale on a mortgage foreclosure. A sale made under proper authority following a levy on the property of a debtor.

executor (m.), executrix (f.)
A person designated by a testator to administer and settle his estate.

executory
That which has yet to be performed.

exemplary damages
See *damages, exemplary*.

exempli gratia *(Lat.)*
For the sake of example. For example. Abbreviated e.g.

ex gratia *(Lat.)*
By grace; gratuitous.

exhume
To disinter.

ex necessitate *(Lat.)*
By necessity.

ex parte *(Lat.)*
Partly; on behalf of. An action by a party in which he has an interest and which may or may not be against an adverse party, e.g., in bankruptcy.

expatriation
The voluntary abandonment of one's country, to become a citizen of another.

expectancy
Being deferred until a future time; an estate is *in expectancy* when the right to possession is postponed to a future time.

expectant right
A right that is *contingent* and not *vested*, based on an anticipated set of circumstances.

expedite
To facilitate; to hasten.

expediter
One who expedites, especially an employee who sees to the smooth flow of materials and goods in a production plant.

ex post facto *(Lat.)*
After the fact.

express
Unambiguous; definite; stated explicitly.

express assumpsit
An undertaking to perform some act, manifested in unmistakable terms.

expressio unius est exclusio alterius *(Lat.)*
The expression of one thing is the exclusion of the other.

express trust
A trust created by unambiguous (express) intent and terms of the *settlor*; as distinguished from an implied trust, which must be deduced from the nature of a transaction.

expungement
Blotting out. Usually in reference to police records on citizens, when an inference might be drawn that for police merely to have a record of a person indicates that the person is a wrongdoer, and hence to maintain the record would be

unjustifiably prejudicial.

ex relatione *(Lat.)*
Upon relation; upon information. Proceedings brought on behalf of the state, but on the information of a person having a private interest in the outcome of the matter.

ex tempore *(Lat.)*
Without preparation.

extenuate
To reduce; to mitigate.

extortion
Obtaining money from another illegally; generally associated with blackmail or with the sale of "protection."

extradition
Upon request, the forcible returning of a criminal to a jurisdiction by another state or by a foreign nation to which the criminal has fled to escape the law.

extra judicum *(Lat.)*
Out of court. Beyond jurisdiction.

extra vires *(Lat.)*
See *ultra vires*.

extrinsic evidence
Evidence not found within the body of a document, contract, or agreement.

face of instrument
The express language of a document, without extrinsic interpretive information or other explanation.

face value
The value of an instrument as can be determined from the language used on the instrument itself, without resorting to external tables or other evidence.

facsimile   An exact copy.

facta sunt potentiora verbis *(Lat.)*
Deeds are stronger than words.

factor
A broker; an agent employed to sell goods entrusted to him by the principal.

failure
Deficiency; lack; ineffectualness. An unsuccessful attempt.

failure of consideration
Where consideration once contemplated and paid diminishes in value. Also, want or lack of consideration.

fair market value
An amount that would induce a willing seller to sell and a willing buyer to buy. Where real property is involved, a fair market value may be arrived at through standard appraisal techniques.

fair use
In copyright law, an imprecise term not expressly recognized by the Copyright Act. Fair use refers to the ways in which a work might be used, the circumstances and purpose of use, and the effect of use on the original copyright holder, as well as other factors, in determining the extent of use before it becomes *plagiarism*.

false imprisonment
A tort consisting of unlawfully detaining, arresting, or constraining a person. Arrest without proper authority.

family car doctrine
A doctrine upheld in certain jurisdictions, maintaining that an owner of a car who provides the car for his family's pleasure and convenience is liable for any negligent driving on the part of family members when they are using the car with his knowledge and consent.

family hotel
A hotel designed for permanent accommodations.

Fannie Mae
See *FNMA*.

fas *(Lat.)*
Right; justice.

fatal
Causing death; capable of defeating, such as a point that is "fatal" to an argument.

fealty
(feudal law) Fidelity; allegiance to a feudal lord.

feasance
A performance; the doing of an act.

featherbedding
The employee practice of limiting production in order to provide more jobs and reduce or avoid unemployment.

fee simple absolute
An unqualified freehold estate. An estate in land that can be conveyed or devised unconditionally and without limitation.

fee tail
A freehold estate of inheritance that is limited to the current holder and heirs of his body, either male or female.

fellow servant rule
The rule that a master, or employer, is not responsible to his servant, or employee, if a fellow servant (employee) causes him harm when the master has exercised proper care to avoid the mishap.

felonious
With intent to commit a felony or a crime.

felony
A serious crime; a crime not a misdemeanor; a crime for which a person can be sent to a state prison.

felony murder
Any homicide committed while carrying out or attempting a felony. Considered first-degree murder.

feme covert
A married woman.

feme sole
A single woman.

fence
(slang) One who knowingly receives stolen property, with the intent to sell it at a profit.

ferae bestiae *(Lat.)*
Wild beasts.

ferae naturae *(Lat.)*
Wild animals. Animals that are naturally wild. The opposite of *domitae naturae.*

ferme
A farm; a rent; a lease.

fetters
Hobbles; shackles for the feet.

ff. (abbrev.)
Following (pages).

FHA
Federal Housing Administration.

FHLBB
Federal Home Loan Bank Board.

fictitious
False; not real.

fictive
Fictitious.

fides *(Lat.)*
Faith, as in phrases *bona fides*, good faith; *mala fides*, bad faith; *uberrima fides*, utmost good faith.

fiduciary
A trustee. Founded upon trust.

fieri facias *(Lat.)*
That you cause to be done. An order to a sheriff to take goods or property from a debtor to satisfy a judgment on behalf of the person to whom a debt is owed. Abbreviated *fi. fa.*

fi. fa. *(Lat. abbrev.)*
Fiere facias.

FIFO
First in, first out. With regard to an inventory, when stock cannot be identified by unit, those items purchased first are regarded as sold first.

filibuster
Tactics to obstruct legislative action, usually through the making of long speeches or the introduction of irrelevant material.

final disposition
A judgment terminating with finality a subject matter before the court, establishing the rights and obligations of the parties to the action.

finder's fee
A fee paid to a person who refers business to another.

firebug
An arsonist; a pyromaniac; one who sets fires.

firm offer
An offer by a merchant to buy or sell goods, in a signed writing, which by its terms gives assurance that it will be held open, unrevokable for lack of consideration during the time stated, and, if no time is stated, for a reasonable time not to exceed three months. Any such term of assurance on a

72

form supplied by the offeree must be separately signed by the offeror. UCC Sec. 2-205.

first impression, case of
A case presenting a question of law never previously arisen in the jurisdiction, and which therefore has no precedent.

fiscal
Concerning or relating to accounts or to the management of money.

fixed asset
An asset basic and necessary to the operation of a business.

fixture
Something that has been affixed to realty, so as to become part of the realty, and which is therefore not readily removable. Something that has been so affixed to realty that its removal could only be effected at great damage either to it or to the realty itself.

flagrante delicto *(Lat.)*
In the very act of committing a crime.

flim-flam
A form of confidence game.

flotsam
Debris floating on the water, after having been cast overboard to lighten a ship, or merely floating on the surface after a ship has sunk. It also refers to bits of floating wreckage. *Flotsam* is often used with *jetsam*, which means debris or wreckage that has sunk or has been washed ashore.

FNMA
Federal National Mortgage Association. "Fannie Mae."

FOB
Free on Board. UCC Sec. 2-309.

forbearance
A delay in taking action to enforce rights; refraining from action.

forced sale
A sale prescribed by law in execution of a judgment.

force majeur
Superior or irresistible force.

forcible detainer
Forcible holding of lands to which one is not entitled, as opposed to rightful possession by the owner.

foreclosure
The enforcement of payment of a debt, by taking and selling the security for the debt. E.g., under a mortgage, a *mortgagee* may take back the mortgaged property from a defaulting *mortgagor*, sell the property, and thereby satisfy the debt.

foreign corporation
A corporation incorporated in another state. As distinguished from a *domestic corporation*, which is incorporated in the same state, and an *alien corporation*, which is incorporated outside the United States or its territories.

foreign jurisdiction
A jurisdiction other than the one referred to.

forensic medicine
Medical knowledge as applied to the law or to the resolution of legal issues. Medical jurisprudence.

forms of action
The various classes of common law personal actions, e.g., assumpsit, case, covenant, debt, detinue, replevin, scire facias, trespass, trover.

fortuitous
By chance; accidental.

forum
A court; the specific court in which an action is brought.

forum non conveniens (Lat.)
A doctrine whereby a court of competent jurisdiction may refuse to entertain a case if it feels that by doing so it might be presenting undue hardship to the defendant. In asserting the doctrine, the court will weigh the relative convenience of the available forums to the parties and the witnesses. *Forum non conveniens* assumes that there is at least one other competent jurisdiction.

forum prorogatum
In international law, the principle that a court's jurisdiction is established by the unconditional acceptance of the forum by the respondent, without which it cannot proceed. Jurisdiction by consent.

foundling home
An orphanage.

four corners
A reference to the face of a written instrument and to the examination and construction of the instrument as a whole.

franchise
A special privilege granted by the government to telephone companies, public services, and the like, to operate as regulated monopolies, or by corporations, for the use of trade names in the marketing of a product.

frank
Free.

franking privilege
The privilege of sending materials through the public mail without paying postage.

fraud
An act of deceit, deception, trickery, or knowing employment of the means to cheat somebody, whether by doing or saying something, or by refraining from doing or

saying something, when deceit follows.

frauds, statute of
Any of various legislative acts, patterned after an English statute of 1677, the force of which is to require certain instruments, primarily those associated with land transfer and certain sales of goods, to be in writing so as to avoid fraud and perjury. See UCC Sec. 2-201.

FRCP
Federal Rules of Civil Procedure.

Free Exercise Clause
The First Amendment guarantee that "Congress shall make no law . . . prohibiting the free exercise [of religion]."

freehold estate
An estate in land, whether in fee or for life.

free on board
Goods sold are to be loaded for shipment without expense to the buyer. Abbreviated FOB. See UCC Sec. 2-309.

friend of the court
See *amicus curiae*.

frivolous
Used when an answer to a pleading is clearly insufficient on its face, failing to controvert material points presented, and may be presumed to have been advanced to delay court action or to embarrass an adversary.

fructus industriales *(Lat.)*
Industrial fruits. Products of labor and industry, such as crops from fields tilled annually, as opposed to *fructus naturales*, which are the products of nature alone, such as minerals, orchard fruit, and young animals.

fructus naturales *(Lat.)*
Natural fruits. Products of nature, such as orchard fruit, minerals, and young animals, as opposed to *fructus industriales*, which are the products of labor, such as from

76

fields tilled annually.

FTC
Federal Trade Commission.

fugues
A form of automatism wherein one unconsciously wanders about, performing involuntary acts. Also, *ambulatory automatism*.

full faith and credit
From the U.S. Constitution, Article IV, Section 1, requiring that a judgment rendered in a foreign jurisdiction has the same effect and obligatory force in other states as it has in the state where handed down.

fungible goods
Those goods that are assumed to be uniform, and hence any one unit is equivalent to any other — e.g., one bushel of wheat is said to be the same as any other bushel of wheat.

futures
Speculative transactions in which there is a nominal contract of sale for delivery at a future time. See UCC Sec. 2-205(2).

future estate
An estate that is not vested at the present time, but is to vest at some time in the future. Includes *remainders* and *reversions*.

FY
Fiscal year.

GAO
General Accounting Office.

gaol *(Br.)*
Jail.

gaoler *(Br.)*
Jailer.

garnishment
A proceeding by which a person's wages or goods in the possession of another are withheld and delivered to a person to whom a debt is owed.

general denial
A pleading denying every material allegation of a complaint.

general issue
A common law answer to a complaint, similar to a general denial.

general judgment
A judgment *in personam*, or against a specific person.

general jurisdiction
Jurisdiction over any controversy that may be brought before a court within legal bounds of a person's rights. As opposed to special or limited jurisdiction.

general power of appointment
A general authority by which the donee may appoint anyone he chooses.

general verdict
A jury verdict of guilty or not guilty, without further elaboration on the specific facts of the case before it.

germane
Related; appropriate; pertinent.

gibbet
The gallows.

gift over
A gift that is made to a person with an interceding ownership by another person. Hence, a gift made from X to Y for life, and then to Z, constitutes a gift over.

gloss
An annotation; an interpretation; an explanation.

good
Valid; lawfully sufficient; collectible.

good cause
With adequate justification; substantial or sufficient legal reason; not arbitrary.

good consideration
Valuable consideration. More precisely, consideration of natural love and affection, as between family members; founded on natural duty.

Good Samaritan Doctrine
Where one encounters another in imminent danger and attempts to aid, the Good Samaritan Doctrine maintains that he may not be held liable for any harm caused to the person except as such harm may be the result of his negligence.

good title
A valid and marketable title; a title free from valid liens, claims, and encumbrances.

gossamer
Light; thin.

government de facto
The government actually in power. See *de facto*.

government de jure
The rightful government. See *de jure*.

Government Organization Manual, United States
See *United States Government Organization Manual*.

grammatica falsa non vitiat chartam (Lat.)
False grammar does not vitiate a deed.

grandfather clause
A clause in licensing, certification, and other arrangements stating that, when new requirements for entering the field are passed, and it is unrealistic to demand that persons

successfully performing in the field should meet the new qualifications, the new criteria will apply only to people applying for admission for the first time. E.g., if for a particular position it is decided that a high school diploma is required, a grandfather clause would excuse those persons already on the job who do not have a diploma from getting one.

grand rights
In dramatic and dramatico-musical compositions, the rights that writers have in dramatic renditions of their works.

grant
To give; to convey; to transfer by deed; to bestow.

grantee
The person to whom a grant is made.

grantor
The person by whom a grant is made.

gratuitous
Free; voluntary; without consideration.

gratuitous guest
A person riding in a vehicle without payment and with the permission and knowledge of the driver.

gratuitous licensee
A visitor, other than one on business, who is not a trespasser.

gratuitous transfer
A transfer made gratis or without consideration.

gravamen
Essence; substance; an injury complained of.

gross income
All income that is taxed. Except for certain death benefits, gifts and inheritances, interest on local obligations, certain compensation for injuries or sickness, social security benefits, and other items as specified by the Code, all

income is includible in gross income.

gross weight
The total weight of goods or an object, including the weight of the container or containers.

ground rent
Value paid for the use of leased land.

Guarantee Clause
Article IV, Section 4, U.S. Constitution: "The United States shall guarantee to every State in this Union a republican form of government, and shall protect each of them against invasion; and on application of the legislature, or of the executive (when the legislature cannot be convened) against domestic violence."

guarantor
One who makes a *guaranty*.

guaranty
A promise to answer for the debt or duty of another, if the latter should fail to perform on a promise.

guest statute
In certain states, statutes that define the limits of care required of a driver toward a gratuitous passenger in his vehicle. Guest statutes do not hold a driver to only a negligence standard. Rather, they speak in terms of "gross negligence" or "reckless disregard" in fixing liability on a driver, thus making it more difficult for a passenger to sue than in states where there are no guest statutes.

HA *(Lat.)*
Hoc Anno. In this year.

habeas corpus *(Lat.)*
You have the body. Nowadays, a writ to secure the release of a person who is being held in prison unlawfully. The writ implies neither guilt nor innocence, but rather it speaks to the issue of due process for imprisonment.

harass
To badger; to disturb persistently.

harbor
To shelter; to protect improperly.

hard case
A case which responds more to the hardship of a party than to true principles of law. The phrase has it that "hard cases do not make good law."

harmless error
An error by a lower court that is not so prejudicial as to have affected an appellant's basic rights, and which therefore does not merit reversal of a judgment.

HB
House Bill. A bill introduced in the House of Representatives.

HC
Habeas corpus (q.v.)

head of household
For tax purposes, a person who is not married at the end of the taxable year and who maintains a household constituting the principal place of abode for some relative. See Code Sec. 2(b)(1) for details.

hearsay
Second-hand evidence. Evidence not from the personal knowledge of the witness, but from another source. Its value depends upon the veracity and competence of its source.

heir
One who inherits property; one who succeeds to an estate by rules of law.

heir by devise
One who succeeds to an estate by will of the decedent.

heir, legal
One who succeeds to an estate by rules of law, based on his

relationship with the decedent.

heir of the body
An heir born to the decedent or a child of an heir born to the decedent. A lineal descendant.

held
Reference to a decision or holding of a court.

hereditament
Something that may be inherited, including both real and personal property.

hereditaments, corporeal
See *corporeal hereditaments*.

hereditaments, incorporeal
See *incorporeal hereditaments*.

Hobson's choice
A choice between two or more objectionable alternatives. Freedom to make a choice where no meaningful choice exists, such as an option between being hanged or going before a firing squad.

hoc *(Lat.)*
This.

Hohfeldian terminology
See *Hohfeld, Wesley Newcomb*.

Hohfeld, Wesley Newcomb (1879–1918)
Law professor and legal theoretician whose analytical jurisprudence redefined basic conceptions of law and who introduced new terminology to present his analyses.

For a brief discussion of Hohfeld's work, see: Walter Wheeler Cook, Hohfeld's Contributions to the Science of Law (1919) 28 Yale Law Journal, 720.

holder in due course
A holder who has taken an instrument under specific conditions, to wit: that the instrument is complete on its

face; that he became the holder of it before it came due, or before it was dishonored, if indeed it was; that he took it in good faith and for value; that at the time it was negotiated to him he was unaware of any infirmity in the instrument or defect in the title of the person from whom he received it.

holdover tenant

A tenant who retains possession of a property after the expiration date of his lease.

holograph

An instrument written entirely in the hand of the person executing it.

holographic will

A will written entirely in the hand of the testator.

home rule

Local self-government.

homestead exemption laws

Laws allowing a homeowner to designate a house and land, with certain limitations, as a homestead, thereby exempting it from execution for his general debts.

homicide

The killing of a human being.

hornbook

A book containing the basic principles of a subject; a primer.

hot cargo clause

A clause in a contract between an employer and a union stating that the employer will not have the union handle materials manufactured or being transferred by an employer with whom there is a labor dispute, or who the union considers unfair to labor. The term "hot cargo" was adopted because such clauses were most often found in Teamsters contracts.

hung jury

A trial jury whose members are unable to arrive at an

agreement in determining a verdict.

ibid *(Lat., abbrev.)*
Ibidem. In the same place. In footnotes, referring to the same work and page as a previous reference.

ICC
Interstate Commerce Commission.

id. *(Lat., abbrev.)*
Idem. The same. In footnotes, referring to the same work as mentioned previously.

i.e. *(Lat.)*
Id est. That is.

ignominy
Dishonor; public disgrace.

ignorantia legis non excusat *(Lat.)*
Ignorance of the law is no excuse.

illusory
Deceptive; deceiving; having false appearances.

illusory promise
A statement that has the appearance of a promise, but that depends upon the will of the promisor, and hence is no promise.

immovables
In property, those things that cannot reasonably be moved, such as buildings, land, and trees. As distinguished from *movables*, or those things that can readily be moved, such as furniture, cut wood, and equipment.

impanel
See *empanel*.

impeach
To charge a public official with misconduct. To establish the untruthfulness of a witness.

impertinent
Irrelevant; without relationship to a particular matter.

implead
To bring a third party into a previously filed lawsuit, on the ground that the third party may be liable to the impleading party for all or part of the judgment to be rendered against the impleading party. See FRCP 14(a).

implied contract
A contract not created by an explicit agreement on the part of the principals but implied by law as may be deduced from circumstances of a transaction or relationship of the parties.

implied trust
A trust that is inferred or implied from circumstances rather than expressed. A trust that is implied by law.

implied warranty
Implication by law of a warranty that goods sold for a particular purpose are fit for the purpose intended. See UCC Sections 2-314 and 2-315.

impossibilium nulla obligatio est *(Lat.)*
There is no obligation to do the impossible.

impression, case of first
A case involving a new question, one never dealt with by the courts. A case without precedent.

improvident
Lacking foresight.

improvidently
In an improvident manner. When a court renders a decision, gives a rule, grants certiorari, and so on, either under a mistaken impression or without adequate consideration, or for any other similar reason that would diminish the

effectiveness of the court, it is said to have acted
improvidently.

impugn
To refute; to attack as untrue; to oppose or challenge.

impute
To attribute, in a negative sense. To charge a person with
knowledge, negligence, or notice of something over which
he has indirect responsibility.

inalienable, unalienable
That which cannot be bought, sold, or transferred. Not
subject to trade. As in the Declaration of Independence,
"... all men ... are endowed by their Creator with certain
unalienable rights. ..."

inapposite
Not relevant or pertinent.

in articulo mortis *(Lat.)*
At the point of death.

in banc
In bank. On the bench. Court proceedings before the judges
of the court in bank, as opposed to proceedings at *nisi prius*,
which would be with only a single judge and a jury.

incarceration
Imprisonment.

inception
Beginning; commencement.

inchoate
Partial; not completed.

inchoate dower
The interest held by a wife in the real property of her
husband, contingent upon her surviving him.

incident to
Belonging to; part of; dependent upon some other thing.

incommunicado
Cut off from communication, such as a prisoner who is kept from communicating with his attorney, family, friends, or others outside the jail or prison.

incompetent
One who is unfit because of minority, insanity, or some other disabling reason. Not legally qualified.

incorporeal hereditament
Something intangible that issues from property, and that may be inherited — e.g., rents, inheritable rights.

incubus
Something oppressive or burdensome.

inculpatory
Tending to establish or fix blame or guilt.

incumbrance
See *encumbrance*.

indebitatus assumpsit
See *assumpsit*.

indefeasible
That which cannot be voided.

indemnify
To compensate; to make good an incurred loss.

indemnity
One party's compensation for loss by another party, primarily economic compensation.

indenture
A written instrument between two parties, called an indenture because the document originally was written twice on a single parchment, which was then cut in half with

a jagged edge, each party retaining half.

indictment
An accusation in writing handed down by a duly sworn grand jury.

indigent
A poor person. A person without property or money.

indispensable party
A party to an action in equity whose interest in the controversy is such that the court cannot proceed without him. See *necessary party*.

indivisible
That which cannot be divided. Inseparable.

indorse
The writing of a name on the back of a document, such as a check, whereby the property in the name written is assigned to another. Also, *endorse*.

indorso *(Lat.)*
On the back.

inducement
In pleading, an explanatory introduction to the main allegations. A motive for doing something.

ineluctable
Inevitable; not to be avoided.

in esse *(Lat.)*
In being; existing.

in extremis *(Lat.)*
At the very end. About to die.

infant
A minor.

in fee

In fee simple. Refers to an estate in *fee simple absolute*, an unqualified freehold estate. Unconditional ownership.

inferior court

A term defining the relation of a court within the hierarchy of a court system. Hence, a court whose decisions are subject to review by a higher, superior court.

in forma pauperis *(Lat.)*

As a pauper. A classification allowing a person to have subpoenas issued and have counsel provided without having to pay, because of poverty.

information

A criminal accusation issued by a competent public officer, differing from an *indictment* in that the latter is issued by a grand jury.

in foro conscientiae *(Lat.)*

In the forum of the conscience. From the moral point of view.

infra *(Lat.)*

Below.

infraction

Violation.

in gross

See *easement in gross*.

in haec verba *(Lat.)*

In these words. By these words.

inherently dangerous

Where an object has in itself the potential for causing harm or destruction, against which precautions must be taken. Dangerous *per se*, without requiring human intervention to produce harmful effects — e.g., explosives.

inheritance
Property acquired through laws of descent and distribution from a person who dies intestate, as distinguished from a *bequest* or *devise*.

in invitum *(Lat.)*
Against the unwilling. Proceedings against a non-consenting party.

injunction
A writ issued by the court in equity directed at a person either to prohibit him from performing some act (preventive injunction) or to command him to perform some act (mandatory injunction), where for some reason the remedy provided by law is inadequate.

injunctive relief
Redress for a wrong or for an injustice, in the form of an *injunction* against the proper party.

in lieu of
In place of; instead of.

in litem *(Lat.)*
For a lawsuit.

in loco parentis *(Lat.)*
In place of a parent.

in medias res *(Lat.)*
In the middle of the thing. To the heart of the matter, without introduction.

in pais
In the country; meaning, not in a court of record.

in pari delicto *(Lat.)*
In equal fault; equally to blame.

in perpetuo *(Lat.)*
In perpetuity. Forever.

inquest
A judicial inquiry.

in re *(Lat.)*
Concerning. In the matter of. A title of a judicial proceeding in which there are no adversaries, but merely some thing, or matter, that requires the court's attention. E.g., a will in probate.

in rem, judgment
A judgment against property, over which the court must have jurisdiction. A judgment in rem can be enforced against any person controlling the object of the action.

in solido *(Lat.)*
As a whole; for the whole. When two or more persons are obliged *in solido* to pay a debt, each is liable for the whole, or entire, payment.

insolvency
The inability of a person to pay his debts as they become due.

instant
Current; present.

instant case
The case being discussed.

instructions, jury
A statement made by a judge to a jury concerning the principles of law that apply in the case the jury is to decide. Jury instructions are given after final arguments by both the prosecution and the defense and just before the jury withdraws to deliberate.

instrument
A formal, written legal document, such as a contract, a deed, or a will.

insufficiency
In equity pleading, an answer that fails to reply to the

material allegations set forth in the complaint.

intangible
That which has no physical quality, such as a right or a sentiment.

integration
In contract, a writing that is accepted by the parties as a final and complete expression of an agreement between the parties.

intendment
The true meaning or intention.

inter alia *(Lat.)*
Among other things.

inter alios *(Lat.)*
Among other persons.

interdiction
Prohibition.

interlocking directorates
When a person serves as a director of two or more corporations, under certain circumstances that work in restraint of trade.

interlocutory
Temporary.

interlocutory judgment
See *judgment, interlocutory*.

internal law
In conflict of law, the laws of a jurisdiction, with the exception of its *choice-of-law* rule.

interpleader
Where two or more persons dispute a claim to something held by a third person who himself claims no interest in it, the third person may file a bill of interpleader to force the

two adverse parties to litigate the matter to determine their individual rights.

Interpol
International Criminal Police Organization.

interposition
Where a state may reject an order from the federal government if it believes that the federal government has exceeded its authority. Based on the Tenth Amendment reservation to the states of those powers not delegated to the federal government.

interrogatories
Written questions posed on behalf of a party to an action to a person having information of interest to the case. The questions must be replied to in writing and under oath. See FRCP 26 and 33.

inter se *(Lat.)*
Among themselves.

intervention
Where a third party not originally a party to a suit claims an interest and enters a case in an effort to protect a right or to assert a claim. See FRCP 24.

inter vivos *(Lat.)*
Between the living—e.g., an "inter vivos" gift, or a gift from one living person to another.

intestacy
The state of dying without having executed a valid will to dispose of all or part of an estate.

intestate
Referring to one who dies without having executed a valid will to dispose of all or part of his estate.

in toto *(Lat.)*
Wholly; entirely.

intra vires *(Lat.)*
Within powers. As opposed to *ultra vires* *(q.v.)*.

intrust
To deliver something to another in trust, with a mutual understanding as to what use is to be made of it and with the belief that the understanding will be honored. Also, *entrust*.

inure
To take effect; to result.

inurement
Use; to a person's benefit.

inventory
A detailed list of all stock held for sale to customers in the regular course of a trade or business.

in ventre sa mere *(Law Fr.)*
In his mother's womb. Referring to an unborn child.

invidious
Offensive.

invitee
A person who by either implied or express invitation goes onto the property of another.

involuntary nonsuit
A nonsuit where the plaintiff either fails to appear or, where appearing, fails to produce evidence on which a jury could find a verdict. A compulsory nonsuit.

ipsissimis verbis *(Lat.)*
In the very same words. In the exact words.

ipso facto *(Lat.)*
By the fact itself.

issue
The point or points to be resolved by a court or jury. If the issues are of law, the court must resolve them. If they are of

fact, they must be determined by the jury. Also, lineal descendants.

issue preclusion
See *collateral estoppel*.

J. (pl. JJ.)
Judge; Justice.

JAG
Judge Advocate General (U.S. Army).

jeopardy
Danger.

jetsam
Debris that has sunk or washed ashore, after having been cast overboard to lighten a ship in danger of sinking. See *flotsam*.

J.N.O.V.
Judgment non obstante veredicto (q.v.).

jobber
One who buys and sells for others.

joinder of claims
When a party asserting a claim to relief as an original claim, a counterclaim, or a cross-claim, joins that claim with other claims that he has against the opposing party. See FRCP 18.

joinder of parties
United as parties to an action all persons who have the same rights or against whom rights are claimed, as either co-plaintiffs or co-defendants. See FRCP 19 and 20.

joint
Combined; shared; united.

joint lives
A designation for the duration of an estate in the name of two or more persons, where the joint lives terminate upon the

death of any one of the persons named.

joint tenants
See *tenants, joint*.

JP
Justice of the Peace.

judge-made law
Where a judge construes in a law an intent that was never contemplated by the legislature. Also, law by precedent.

judgment creditor
A creditor in whose favor a judgment on a credit has been rendered, but who has not yet received payment from the *judgment debtor*.

judgment debtor
A debtor against whom a judgment has been rendered, but who has yet to make payment of the debt to the *judgment creditor*.

judgment, estoppel by
An *estoppel* imposed by a valid judgment previously rendered by a competent court.

judgment in personam
A judgment against a specific person, over whom the court must have jurisdiction, compelling him to comply with the demands of the court.

judgment, interlocutory
A judgment made during the course of a proceeding to settle some point which must be determined before continuing. It does not finally determine the case, but merely disposes of accessory contentions.

judgment non obstante veredicto (Lat.)
Judgment notwithstanding the verdict. A judgment given in favor of one party notwithstanding, or in spite of, a jury finding for the opposing party. Abbreviated J.N.O.V.

judicial action
Court action.

judicial comity
The principle that a court in one jurisdiction will give effect to the decisions of equal and superior courts in other jurisdictions, as a matter of practice rather than as a matter of law.

judicial errors
Errors of the court during a proceeding, or in rendering a judgment, that require a reversal or a revision of the opinion.

judicial notice
Court acceptance of certain facts without proof.

jura eodem modo destituuntur quo constituunter *(Lat.)*
Laws are abrogated by the same means by which they are constituted.

jura fiscalia *(Lat.)*
(Great Britain) Fiscal rights. The rights of the Exchequer.

jurat
A statement at the end of an affidavit acknowledging the date, place, and person before whom the affidavit was sworn.

jure uxoris *(Lat.)*
The right of a wife.

jurisdiction
The extent of the legitimate authority of the court. The authority of the court. The right to decide a question properly presented to the court.

jurist
An expert in the field of law.

jury instructions
See *instructions*.

jus disponendi *(Lat.)*
The right of disposing, i.e., the right to alienate. One may give up possession of something and still maintain the *jus disponendi*.

jus mariti *(Lat.)*
The right of the husband.

jus tertii *(Lat.)*
The right of a third party.

justiciable
That which can properly be determined in a judicial proceeding.

kangaroo court
A mock court. A court devoid of legality.

KB
King's Bench *(q.v.)*.

kickback
Money or valuables given to a public or corporate employee for his personal use, for awarding in his official capacity a favor or a contract to another person or corporation.

killing by misadventure
The accidental killing of a person while engaged in a lawful activity.

King's Bench
In England, the supreme court of common law, called King's Bench because the king used to sit on it. Called Queen's Bench during the reign of a queen.

kite
Negotiable paper that has no value, written for the purpose of temporarily maintaining credit or of raising money.

kiting
Issuing a check or other instrument against an account that

cannot cover it, on the expectation that by the time the accounting is completed there will be sufficient funds in the account to cover it.

kleptomania
An irresistible propensity to steal.

laches
Delay for sufficient time as to assume acquiescence. Where a person neglects to assert his rights, not as measured by a statute of limitations but as justice would require in any given case.

lame duck
An elected office holder who is to be succeeded by another, between the time of election and the date that his successor is to take office. A speculator in stock who has over-bought and cannot meet his commitments.

Lame Duck Amendment
The Twentieth Amendment to the U.S. Constitution, abolishing the short congressional term.

landlord
One who leases or rents land to another.

Landrum-Griffin Act
A federal statute that subjects to federal regulation the internal affairs of unions, as the result of abuses from loose fiscal and administrative controls within some unions. Also known as the Labor Management Reporting and Disclosure Act of 1959, or LMRDA.

Lanham Act
A federal statute (1946) that concerns the laws of trade and service marks, trade names, and related areas.

larceny
Felonious stealing of another's goods without color of right and without permission, intending to deprive the rightful owner of further possession. Thievery.

last resort, court of
A court from which there is no appeal.

latent defect
A defect in salable goods, hidden and not readily discoverable upon inspection. Opposite of *apparent defect*.

lateral support
The right to have one's land supported by the surrounding land.

Law French
The Norman French language of William the Conquerer, introduced to England after the Norman invasion of 1066.

law of the case
A doctrine acknowledging a previous decision on a subject-matter; the practice of courts generally to refuse to re-open a case once settled.

leading case
A case setting a precedent that is considered to establish a principle of law.

leading question
A question framed in such a way as to provide or suggest the answer sought or expected. E.g., "On the afternoon in question you were in your office, were you not?"

ledger
A business account book.

legacy
A disposition of personal property by will; a *bequest*, as distinguished from a *devise*, which disposes of real property.

legal consideration
Consideration deemed lawful and recognized as legally binding.

legal fiction
An assumption of fact made by the court as a basis for the

resolution of a controversy, although it is not supported by fact.

legal title
A title enforceable in court as regards ownership of property, but not necessarily establishing an interest for profit, benefit, or advantage in the property.

legatee
One to whom a legacy is given.

legatee, residuary
A person receiving the residue of a personal estate, after specific legacies are satisfied.

legislative intent
Legislative purpose in enacting a statute. Referred to when courts attempt to construe a statute which is either ambiguous or inconsistent with another statute or a more satisfactory construction.

legitime
In the civil law, that part of a parent's estate that by law must pass to the children, providing there is no legal reason why it should not.

lesion
Damage; injury.

lessee
The person to whom a lease is made.

lessor
One who grants a lease.

letters rogatory
A request by a court of one jurisdiction to a court of another jurisdiction, that a witness be examined by interrogatories accompanying the request. See 185 F. Supp. 832.

levy
Assess, exact, or impose, such as to levy a tax. To begin, such

102

as to levy war.

lex domicilii *(Lat.)*
In conflict of laws, the law of the domicile.

lex fori *(Lat.)*
In conflict of laws, the law of the forum.

lex loci *(Lat.)*
The law of the place; the law of the place where a contract was made or an act committed.

lex loci contractus *(Lat.)*
In conflict of laws, the law of the place of a contract.

lex loci delicti *(Lat.)*
In conflict of laws, the law of the place of the wrong.

lex rei sitae *(Lat.)*
In conflict of laws, the law of the place of the thing (in dispute).

Lex Salica *(Lat.)*
Salic Law. Generally, a reference to a provision in a body of laws from 5th century France, the thrust of which provision was that females could not inherit land, and hence, by extension, succession to the crown of France could only be through the male line.

liable
Responsible; answerable.

libel
The common law crime of writing a malicious defamation, tending to injure someone's reputation or subject him to ridicule. Today extended to include otherwise recorded (in writing, on film, on tape) defamatory remarks. Unlike most forms of *slander*, libel is actionable without proof of actual damage.

libellus *(Lat.)*
Diminutive of *liber*, book; hence, a little book. Root of the word libel.

license
Permission or authority to do something that would be unlawful or wrong to do in the absence of permission or authority.

licensee
A person who holds a license; one who is licensed.

lien
An incumbrance upon a property, in the form of a claim or charge for payment of a debt.

lienee
A person whose property is subject to a lien.

lien, mechanics'
See *mechanics' lien*.

lienor
One who holds a lien.

life estate
An estate in land limited in duration by the life of some person, whether the holder of the land or a third party.

life tables
Statistical tables showing life expectancy of persons of different ages.

limitation, words of
Words in a conveyance referring to the duration of the estate.

liquidated
Ascertained; established; fixed; settled.

liquidated damages
The amount established by the parties to a contract which

must be paid, by one or either of the parties, in the event of a default or a breach.

lis pendens
A pending suit.

lis pendens notice
Public announcement of a suit pending regarding certain property, as notice to anybody who would buy the property that it is subject to a claim.

litigant
A person who is a party to litigation; a party to a lawsuit.

litigate
To contend in court, either as plaintiff or as defendant.

litigious
Prone to become involved in lawsuits; said of a person who brings many lawsuits.

littoral rights
The rights of a shore-property holder, by virtue of holding property bordering a sea or lake.

livery of seisin
A common law ceremony whereby possession of lands was transferred from grantor to grantee.

L. J.
Lord Justice.

LMRDA
Labor Management Reporting and Disclosure Act of 1959. Also known as the Landrum-Griffin Act (q.v.).

local action
An action on real property; an action against a locality. Actions that of necessity must be brought in a specific place.

local option
Local regulation of the sale of alcoholic beverages, usually in reference to prohibition or restriction.

locus poenitentiae *(Lat.)*
Place of repentance. A point, place, or chance for a person to withdraw from a contemplated agreement, before agreement and responsibility are actually fixed. Also, a point at which one may withdraw from the commission of a criminal act, or renounce intention to commit a criminal act, before it is carried out.

locus sigilli *(Lat.)*
The place of the seal. The place on a written instrument where a seal is to be affixed, once the instrument is executed. Abbreviated *l.s.*

long arm statute
A statute allowing a court to obtain jurisdiction over a defendant located outside the normal jurisdiction of the court.

long-term capital gains and losses
Gains and losses on sale or exchange of capital assets that have been held for more than 6 months. See Code Sec. 1222.

l.s. (abbrev.)
Locus sigilli.

lucre
Profit; gain. Usually with a negative connotation, referring to ill-gotten gain.

magistrate
A public officer; a justice of the peace.

magna culpa *(Lat.)*
Great fault or blame. Gross negligence.

mailbox rule
In contracts by correspondence (i.e., by post, telegraph, and

the like), a rule holding that once a contract is accepted, executed, and returned by whatever means are appropriate, the offeror cannot revoke it, nor can the offeree reject it, and the risks of transmission fall to the offeror.

maim
To cripple; to injure a person's limb.

maintainor
One who as a third party interferes in a suit in which he has no interest, to aid one of the parties against the other with money or advice.

maintenance
The offense committed by a maintainor.

major
One no longer a minor; a person who is of age.

majority
The condition of being of age; no longer a minor.

mala fides *(Lat.)*
Bad faith.

malefactor
One who has committed some crime.

malfeasance
The doing of an evil act.

malice
Evil intent.

malice aforethought
With a contemplated evil intention, although not necessarily with an intention to produce the eventual result.

malicious
With malice.

malicious mischief
Intentional destruction of another's personal property.

malpractice
Professional misconduct, either because of unreasonable incompetence or because of malicious design. Applied primarily to the medical and legal professions.

malum in se *(Lat.)*
Wrong in itself. An act which is morally wrong, independent of any statute that may declare it wrong, is said to be *malum in se*. See *malum prohibitum*.

malum prohibitum *(Lat.)*
Prohibited wrong. An act made wrong because it is prohibited by a statute, although it may not be evil in itself. See *malum in se*.

mandamus *(Lat.)*
We command. A writ issued by a competent court to a public official, commanding him to perform some act that it is his duty to perform as an official.

mandate
A command; an order.

mandatory
Imperative; that which commands.

manifest
Evident; obvious; unmistakable.

Mann Act
The White Slave Traffic Act (1910). An act making it unlawful for anybody to transport women or girls across state lines "for the purpose of prostitution or debauchery, or for any other immoral purpose." After Congressman James R. Mann.

manslaughter
The unpremeditated unlawful killing of another. Unlawful killing without malice.

manumission
The liberating of a slave.

mark
A sign, usually an X, as a substitute for the signature of a person unable to write his name.

martial law
Military law.

master, special
A court-appointed official who is empowered to represent the court in a transaction, to determine certain facts in a case, and so on.

material
Important; substantial.

material allegation
In a pleading, an allegation that is necessary to a claim or a defense.

materialman
A person furnishing construction materials.

materialmen's lien
See *mechanics' lien*.

maternal
Belonging to or coming from the mother.

matter in pais
Fact that is not a matter of record.

matter of record
A matter that is ascertainable and provable by a record of the court.

maxim
A universally accepted general statement of law.

mayhem
To deprive a person of the function of a bodily part necessary for his defense in a fight, whether an arm, a leg, an eye, or a front tooth, etc., but not a nose, or a jawtooth, or other bodily part not associated with one's defense.

mechanics' lien
A lien by statute, on behalf of a person who has furnished labor, money, or material for the improvement of another person's property, whether personal or real, and that attaches to the property. Also, *materialmen's lien*.

media nox *(Lat.)*
Midnight.

medias res
See *in medias res*.

mediate data
Data from which facts can reasonably be inferred.

mediate testimony
See *secondary evidence*.

medical jurisprudence
See *forensic medicine*.

medley
A mêlée; an affray.

member
A part of the body, particularly a limb.

mens rea *(Lat.)*
Guilty mind; criminal intent.

merchant seaman
A seaman on a privately owned vessel.

meretricious
Pertaining to unlawful sexual relations.

merger
In procedure, consolidation or fusion of causes of action or parties to an action.

merits, judgment on the
Resolution of a case, based on pleadings and evidence as heard in court.

mesne
Intermediate; middle.

mesne profits
In an action of ejectment, the value of the property for the period during which it was unlawfully held.

messuage
A dwelling-house.

metes and bounds
A system of land description by distances, terminal points, and angles (metes — terminal points; bounds — boundaries).

mineral rights
Interest in and rights to the minerals on a property.

Miranda Rule
When a person is taken into custody, and prior to any interrogation, he must be warned that he has the right to remain silent, that any statement he makes may be used against him, that he has the right to speak to an attorney, and that if he cannot afford an attorney one will be appointed for him if he so desires. Unless these warnings are given or the rights are waived, the Miranda Rule maintains that no evidence obtained from an interrogation is allowed in court. Miranda v. Arizona, 384 U.S. 346 (1966).

mirror image rule
In contract, the rule that an acceptance must be a "mirror image" of an offer, and free from implied terms.

miscreant
An unbeliever. One guilty of criminal or vicious behavior.

misdemeanant
One guilty of a misdemeanor.

misdemeanor
An offense that is not a felony and that is punishable by a fine or a jail sentence of short duration.

misfeasance
The improper or injurious performance of some act which in itself is lawful.

misjoinder
The improper joinder of claims or parties to a lawsuit. See FRCP 21.

mislaid property
Property deliberately put someplace by its rightful owner, which place is then forgotten. Such property is not considered lost.

misnomer
A name wrongly used for an individual or a corporation. When the correct party can be ascertained, a misnomer will not render void a contract or a legacy.

misprision of felony
Concealing a felony of another, although one is not an accessory to it.

misprision of office
Neglect or maladministration of one's office; failing in one's official duties, to the degree of an expression of contempt for one's office.

mistrial
A trial that for some reason has not been carried through to a verdict. The most common cause of a mistrial is a hung jury, although other reasons constituting error prejudicial to the defendant could also invalidate the judicial process (e.g.,

death of a juror).

mitigate
To alleviate; to diminish or reduce.

mitigation
Reduction. A lessening in the amount or severity of a penalty or punishment.

mitigating circumstances
Those circumstances that would favor an accused individual and that would permit either a reduction in the charge against him or a more lenient sentence than would ordinarily be expected for the crime for which he has been found guilty.

M'Naghten Rule
A test of criminal responsibility, stating that if a person commits a criminal act and does not know what he is doing, and if he is not aware of the nature and quality of his act, he may not be held responsible.

m.o. *(Lat., abbrev.)*
Modus operandi. Manner of operation.

modus operandi *(Lat.)*
Manner of operation. A particular technique, a set of circumstances, or the specific characteristics of a person's actions; usually in reference to the methods employed by a criminal.

moiety
Half.

moot
Pretend; not genuine.

moral turpitude
Conduct not in keeping with good moral principles. Acts of baseness, vileness, or depravity in one's duties, contrary to customary rule and right. See ABA Code of Professional Responsibility DR1-102 (A) (3) Fn. 13.

morganatic marriage
A marriage between a nobleman and a woman of inferior station, carrying with it certain legal ramifications regarding inheritances.

mortgage
A duly executed written instrument creating a lien upon real property as security for a debt.

mortgagee
A party lending money who receives a mortgage for property as security for payment of the debt. The lender on a mortgage.

mortgagor
A person who borrows money and gives a mortgage on property as security for the debt. The borrower on a mortgage.

motion
An application made to a court to obtain a rule or order directing some act to be done in favor of the applicant.

movables
Personal property. Those things that may reasonably be moved, such as furniture, cut wood, and equipment. As distinguished from *immovables*, or those things that cannot readily be moved, such as buildings, land, and trees.

movant
One who makes a motion before the court.

Ms.
Manuscript.

mulct   A fine.

multilateral
Many sided; with or on many sides.

multitial
Legal relations *in rem*. See *Hohfeld*.

muniments
Written instruments evidencing ownership of land.

mutatis mutandi *(Lat.)*
With necessary changes in points of detail. I.e., matters will remain generally the same, with only substitutions of names and the like, such as would not distort any of the substantive meaning.

mutual insurance company
An insurance company whose policyholders form an association of contributors. Policy premiums are deposited in a fund, against which claims are made and from which indemnities are paid.

mutuality of contract
Reciprocity of obligation, indicating a binding contract. Binding obligation of performance resting on all principals to a contract.

mutual mistake
A misunderstanding of the same matter on the part of both parties to a contract, where the contract unintentionally embodies an erroneous expression of agreement.

named insured
The person whose name appears on an insurance policy for health, life, or property. A policyholder.

NASA
National Aeronautics and Space Administration.

national bank
A bank created under a federal, or national charter.

natural person
A human being, as distinguished from an artificial person, such as a corporation.

NB *(Lat.)*
Nota bene. Note well; observe.

N.D.
Northern District. Refers to a state's district court.

neat cattle
Cows, calves, bulls, or steers, at the exclusion of all other cattle. Bovines.

Necessary and Proper Clause
Article I, Section 8, Clause 18, U.S. Constitution: "The Congress shall have the power . . . (18) To make all laws which shall be necessary and proper for carrying into execution the foregoing powers, and all other powers vested in this Constitution by the government of the United States, or in any department or officer thereof."

necessary party
A party to an action in equity who has an interest in the controversy, but which interest is not so great that it is not separable from that of an *indispensable party* to the action.

nefas *(Lat.)*
Unjust; wrong.

negative averment
An averment in which some negative is used. An averment in the negative.

negative covenant
A covenant by which the servient estate is obliged not to perform a specific act, or is obliged to refrain from committing some act.

negative pregnant
A denial that implies an affirmation of a substantial fact.

116

negligence
Failure to exercise ordinary care or caution under a particular set of circumstances.

nemine contradicente *(Lat.)*
No one dissenting.

nemine dissentiente *(Lat.)*
Nobody dissenting. Unanimous.

nemo dat quod non habet *(Lat.)*
No one can give [gives] what he does not have.

nemo est supra leges *(Lat.)*
No one is above the law.

nemo potest plus juris ad alium transferre quam ipse habet *(Lat.)*
No one can transfer a greater right to another than he himself has.

nepotism
Patronage of one's relatives by providing them employment or position.

net
Free from all charges, expenses, commissions, fees, etc., such as net costs or net profits; after all attending expenses have been paid; weight excluding the weight of the container.

new matter
In pleading, facts not previously alleged.

next friend
In a proceeding, one acting on behalf of another who is legally disabled, such as an infant, without being regularly appointed by the court.

nexus *(Lat.)*
A connection; a link in a series.

nisi *(Lat.)*
Unless.

nisi prius court
A court that conducts trials with judge and jury, as distinguished from appellate courts.

NLRA
National Labor Relations Act.

NLRB
National Labor Relations Board.

nolle prosequi *(Lat.)*
An acknowledgement by a plaintiff or a prosecutor that he will not further prosecute either part or all of a pending case.

nolo contendere *(Lat.)*
I will not contest. In a criminal action, a plea amounting to a plea of guilty, without actual admission of guilt.

nominal
Not real or substantial; in name only.

non compos mentis *(Lat.)*
Not of sound mind. Insane.

nonconforming uses
Uses which under zoning provisions in force for an area are unlawful, but which are allowed as exceptions. E.g., a zoning ordinance excluding all businesses is adopted after a business is already established. As an existing use, although not conforming to the zoning ordinance, the business may continue to operate in that location.

nondisclosure
Failure to disclose.

nonfeasance
Nonperformance or failure to perform an act that one is duty-bound to perform.

non obstante veredicto *(Lat.)*
Notwithstanding the verdict. Abbreviated N.O.V. See *judgment non obstante veredicto*.

nonsuit
A judgment against a plaintiff when he fails to prove his case or fails to appear in court. Not a *judgment on the merits*.

no-strike clause
A clause put into labor contracts as a concession to management, whereby a union relinquishes its right to strike.

notary public
A minor public official whose duty it is to perform certain public functions, such as administer oaths, witness signatures, and acknowledge deeds.

notice of lis pendens
See *lis pendens notice*.

notice to produce
A lawful written notice requiring the adversary in an action to produce a certain document at trial.

notorious
Common knowledge; known to all.

N.O.V.
Non obstante veredicto (q.v.).

novation
The substitution of a new contract for an earlier one, which is thereupon extinguished. The effect is to release the old debt in favor of creating a new one.

NP
Notary public. *Or*, nisi prius *(q.v.)*.

n.s.
In journal citations, indicates "new series."

NSA
National Security Agency.

NSF
National Science Foundation. *Or,* not sufficient funds.

nude pact
See *nudum pactum*.

nudum pactum *(Lat.)*
A bare agreement; a promise not supported by consideration, and therefore not enforceable.

nugatory
Ineffectual; futile.

nullify
To void; to render invalid.

nullity
Nothing.

nunc dimittis *(Lat.)*
Now you let depart. A departure or farewell, particularly from life. A dismissal.

nunc pro tunc *(Lat.)*
Now for then. Acts performed with a retroactive effect.

nuncupative will
An oral declaration intended by the testator to serve as a will, made shortly before death but later reduced to writing by one of the witnesses.

OAS
Organization of American States.

oath helper
See *wager of law*.

obiter
In passing; incidentally.

obiter dictum *(Lat., pl. dicta)*
Something said in passing. Words in a written judicial opinion not necessary to the decision, but as general comment of the judge in considering the case.

obligee
One on whose behalf an obligation exists.

obligor
One bound to perform an obligation.

obloquy
Blame; censure; reproach.

obstante *(Lat.)*
Withstanding.

obstruction of justice
Any act intended to prevent or deter the court from proceeding in an orderly way, either by interference with witnesses, false statements to investigators, destruction of documents, or any other deliberate effort.

odium
Hatred; general ill-feeling against someone.

OEO
Office of Economic Opportunity.

offset
A counterclaim; a set-off.

of record
Officially recorded.

ombudsman
A public official who has broad powers to investigate official actions or inactions that aggrieve citizens and to take or recommend corrective measures.

on all fours
A case that squares with another in facts and legal issues is said to be on all fours with the other case.

onerous
Burdensome. In contract, when one party's obligations far exceed his advantages, the agreement is said to be *onerous*.

onus
Burden; encumbrance.

open shop
A shop where both union and nonunion employees work; contrast *closed shop*.

operative words
In a deed, those words that carry out the main intent or define the transaction meant to be effected.

opinion
The reasons given by a court for reaching a decision. Rationale for a judgment.

opprobrious
Infamous; not worth of respect.

option contract
A contract supported by consideration by which a person holds open a right to buy on terms stated for a specific period. The offeror may not withdraw, revoke, or revise the terms of the offer for the period of the option.

order to show cause
A court order made *ex parte* citing a party to appear in court to show cause as to why a rule sought should not be made final. Also, *rule nisi*; rule to show cause.

ordinance
An enactment of a municipal legislative body.

organic law
Fundamental law of a state, nation, or dependency,

organizing the government and establishing the basic legal institutions by which the government is to function.

original jurisdiction
Jurisdiction to hear a case and to try it on the facts, as opposed to *appellate jurisdiction*, which involves a review power.

output contract
A contract in which a buyer agrees to purchase from a manufacturer his entire output of a particular item. See *requirements contract*.

outside salesman
A salesman whose charge it is to travel, away from the employer's place of business, and to solicit business for the employer. See Code Sec. 62(2)(D).

overreach
In contract, when a party in a superior bargaining position requires unfair concessions from the party in an inferior bargaining position, he is said to overreach.

overrule
For a superior court to void a lower court opinion by holding an opposite opinion.

pais
Country.

pais, trial per
Trial by jury.

palpable
Obvious; evident.

paramount title
A title that is better than the one with which it is compared, usually in the sense that the paramount title has seniority, or dates from a time prior to the other title.

parcenary
The condition of holding land by parceners, before an inheritance is divided among joint heirs.

parcener
A joint heir.

parens patriae *(Lat.)*
Father of the country.

pares *(Lat.)*
Equals.

pari mutuel
In betting, where the winners take from the total amount bet, in proportion to the amount that each has bet, less a percentage that goes to the office conducting the betting.

pari passu *(Lat.)*
Equally; without preference.

parol
Speech; oral; not written.

parole
Release of a prisoner from prison prior to a completion of his sentence, and under conditions which, if not met, will require his return to prison to serve out his term.

parol evidence rule
When two parties reduce an oral agreement to an unambiguous written instrument, the document cannot be modified by oral evidence.

parol promise
A simple contract; a verbal promise.

partial eviction
Where the possessor of a property is evicted from only part of a property.

particulars
Details; items of an account.

particulars, bill of
An account of the items of a claim. A plaintiff's informal statement of a cause of action or a defendant's set-off.

party
A person who directly takes part in a legal proceeding or transaction.

passim *(Lat.)*
Throughout. General reference to a work.

patent
A grant of privilege or property by the government. A conveyance whereby the government transfers land title. Also, apparent, obvious.

patent defect
A defect in goods that is readily observable upon inspection.

paternal
Belonging to or coming from the father.

paucital
Legal relations in personam. See *Hohfeld*.

payee
The person to whom something has been, is, or is to be paid.

pecuniary
Monetary.

pejoration
A worsening.

pelf, pelfe
Ill-gotten gains; booty.

penal
In regard to punishment.

pendency
Being pendent; after beginning and prior to terminating.

pendente lite *(Lat.)*
Pending a suit. While a suit is in progress.

pendent jurisdiction
Where a plaintiff has both a federal claim and a state claim against a particular defendant, with permission of the federal court he may bring action on both claims in the federal forum, and thereby avoid piecemeal litigation.

per autre vie
For another life. For as long as another, specified, person is alive.

per capita *(Lat.)*
By the head. In the law of descent, a method of dividing an intestate estate whereby each individual is given an equal share, without reference to his line of descent. As opposed to *per stirpes*.

percipient
Perceiving; one who perceives, or sees something.

per curiam *(Lat.)*
By the court. By the entire court, as opposed to by a single judge.

peremptory
Arbitrary; final; decisive.

peremptory challenge
A challenge to a prospective juror, in jury selection, disqualifying him from being empaneled for no stated reason. The number of peremptory challenges varies and is established by statute.

perfect
Complete; without defect.

perfidy
Breach of faith or trust.

performance
Fulfillment on a contract or a promise.

performance, specific
Performance on a contract according to the agreed-upon terms. As a remedy, one may sue for specific performance, as opposed to suing for damages or other compensation for nonperformance.

perjury
To assert something that one knows is not true, in connection with a judicial proceeding. To wilfully give false testimony or swear falsely to a document.

perm. (abbrev.)
Permanent.

per metas et bundas *(Lat.)*
By *metes and bounds (q.v.).*

permissive
Allowable.

peroration
Bombastic oratory.

perquisites
Profits incidental to an office, other than salary or fees.

per quod *(Lat.)*
Whereby.

per se *(Lat.)*
By himself, herself, itself. In itself; alone.

personalty
Personal property.

persona non grata *(Lat.)*
Unwelcome person. A person who is unacceptable, generally for some defect in attitude or comportment.

per stirpes *(Lat.)*
By roots; by stock. In the law of descent, a method of dividing an intestate estate whereby a group of individuals take whatever their deceased ancestor would have received. As opposed to *per capita* (*q.v.*).

petition
A written application for redress.

petitioner
One initiating an appeal to a higher court, after having lost in a lower court. Appellant. One who petitions the court.

petty theft
Petty larceny. Theft of something of little value.

PHA
Public Housing Administration.

piercing the corporate veil
In cases involving fraud or unjust enrichment, where the court refuses to recognize a corporation as an entity separate from those responsible for corporate activity, holding the corporation's *alter ego* (*q.v.*) liable, the court is said to pierce the corporate veil.

plagiarism
The taking of another's literary property, in whole or in part, and advancing it as one's own, whether or not for profit.

plain meaning rule
A rule stating that wherever a statute is unambiguous on its face, and where it can be construed in only one way, the court will allow no abstruse construction for purposes of a

128

case. Of course, whether a statute is so clearly stated as to admit only a single construction is for the court to decide.

plaintiff
A person who brings a lawsuit.

plaintiff in error
One who by appeal seeks a review of a judgment. An appellant.

plat
A map drawn to scale of an area, such as a municipality, on which lots, streets, and other features are recorded, with appropriate measurements and boundaries.

plea
A pleading in a legal action.

plea in abatement
A plea that does not answer the merits of a complaint, but that disputes the manner, place, or time in which action is brought.

plea in bar
A plea that absolutely defeats a plaintiff's action.

plenary
Complete; full.

plottage
A term used in appraising land value, by combining a number of smaller lots adjoining one another and under a single owner to arrive at a total value for the large tract.

poll
An individual; a list of registered voters.

polling the jury
To question jurors one by one in open court to require them to voice their verdict.

129   **polls**   Voting place.

poll tax
A tax of a fixed amount levied on each individual, without regard to his ability to pay. In certain states a payment of a poll tax was at one time a prerequisite to voting. The 24th Amendment (1964) abolished all poll taxes as they related to voting.

polygamy
Having more than one husband or wife at the same time.

possessory action
An action to gain possession of real property, usually brought by a landlord to evict a *holdover tenant*.

postea
At common law, a formal record of *nisi prius* proceedings, endorsed by the judge and delivered to the successful party following final disposition of the case.

post mortem *(Lat.)*
After death. An examination of a dead body to determine the cause of death. An autopsy.

power of attorney
Authority, or a letter of authority, for a person to act as agent for the *grantor*.

prayer
That part of a pleading that states a demand for specific relief, and the form or amount of that relief. See FRCP 8(a).

preamble
Introduction.

precatory
Expressing a request, wish, or recommendation, but falling short of a command, as precatory words in a will or a trust

pre-empt
To appropriate or take by pre-emption.

pre-emption
The act of doing or the right to do something before somebody else does it.

preferential debts
Those debts that in bankruptcy have priority, or that must be satisfied before others.

preferred stock
Corporate stock that enjoys certain priority rights, such as the right to a certain percentage of dividends prior to payment to holders of other classes of stock. Preferred stock may also be given preference to corporate assets upon dissolution of the corporation.

prejudice, without
Negotiations, preliminary agreements, offers, admissions, and judgments are said to be carried out or made without prejudice when they are carried out or made at no risk to the parties that they may thereby be waiving or losing privileges or rights. The term "with prejudice" as applied to a judgment of dismissal, refers to a conclusive judgment adverse to the plaintiff, just as if the action had been tried to a final decision.

premeditation
Deliberation; prior consideration.

prepayment penalty
A money sum, usually a percentage of the remaining principal, charged a debtor for the privilege of paying a debt in advance of the date of maturity.

preponderance of evidence
Of greater weight or sufficiency; adequate to overcome doubt and to dispel speculation.

prerogative
An exclusive privilege or advantage held by a person in a particular office or position.

prescription
Acquisition of rights in or title to property through long-term uninterrupted use or enjoyment.

presentment
A grand jury statement, addressed to the court and based on its own knowledge, that it believes that a crime has been committed and that a particular individual named in the presentment is responsible.

presumed grant, doctrine of
A fictitious grant that is established by the presumption of a title by prescription. A doctrine used to quiet title to land adversely held. See *adverse possession*.

presumption of innocence
The consideration that one is innocent of any misdeed until the contrary is established by the evidence.

presumptive
Founded on presumption; assumed.

preterlegal
Beyond the law; not legal.

pretermit
To neglect.

pretermitted heir
A rightful heir that by mistake on the part of the testator has been inadvertently excluded from a will. E.g., a child born after the preparation of a will.

prima facie *(Lat.)*
At first sight; on its face.

prima facie case
A case based on evidence which, if not explained or contradicted, is sufficient to determine an outcome adverse to the defendant.

132

primogeniture
First-born; seniority by birth.

primus inter pares *(Lat.)*
First among equals.

principal
One in a position of authority; a person acting in his own behalf; a party to a contract or to an action.

privileged relations
Relations between persons that would exempt them from being forced to testify on any communications with one another, or on information one might have about the other as the result of such relations — e.g., lawyer/client; priest/penitent.

Privileges and Immunities Clause
Fourteenth Amendment, Section I, U.S. Constitution: "No State shall make or enforce any law which shall abridge the privileges or immunities of citizens of the United States. . . ."

privity
A situation in which two or more persons hold such an interest in something that one of them representing a legal interest would amount to representation of the other or others. Mutual or successive relationship to the same right or property. Identity of interest.

probable cause
Reasonable cause; cause as supported by circumstances.

probate
The proving of a will. Proof before a proper authority that a will is authentic and that it is the last will and testament of the deceased.

probity
Honesty.

pro bono publico *(Lat.)*
For public good; for the general welfare. Indicates where an attorney accepts a case for either a reduced fee or no fee at all, in service to the public.

procedural law
Law governing procedure or practice in legal matters. Also, *adjective law*.

process
A summons.

process server
An official of the court who delivers a summons.

pro confesso *(Lat.)*
As confessed.

produce
To present; to exhibit.

profit a prendre
A type of easement, being a right to take something produced by or on the land, such as minerals or timber (but not running water).

pro forma *(Lat.)*
As a matter of form.

pro hac vice *(Lat.)*
For this occasion.

prohibition, writ of
A writ issued to a person directing him not to do something which the court is informed he is about to do.

prolix
Longwinded; verbose.

prolixity
Being prolix; making superfluous statements.

134

promisee
One to whom a promise is made.

promisor
One who makes a promise.

promissory estoppel
Where a promise which could reasonably be expected to induce some action by a promisee, and such action is taken, the promise is binding if it would work an injustice not to have it be binding.

promissory note
A written promise to pay a specific sum under the conditions of time, place, and other circumstances, as agreed.

promulgate
To make public; to officially announce publicly.

proponent
The person offering a will for probate, as opposed to any contestants of the will.

proprietary
Having to do with ownership.

pro rata *(Lat.)*
Proportionately; by proportion.

prospectus
A corporation's statement regarding an issue of company stocks, debentures, or other securities, published as an invitation to investors.

pro tanto *(Lat.)*
For so much; to that extent.

prothonotary
Generally, the clerk of a court.

provisional remedy
A remedy for an immediate circumstance; an injunction.

proviso
Being provided; a condition or provision.

proximo
Next.

proxy
One appointed to represent another, generally at a meeting where voting is presumably to take place.

publication of service
Printing a summons in a newspaper under prescribed conditions and with certain limitations, as a way of serving process.

public house
A tavern; an inn.

publici juris *(Lat.)*
Of public right. Used in reference to rights that are universal, and not reserved to individuals or classes of individuals. E.g., the right to light and air; the state.

publicist
Primarily, an expert in international law.

public policy
A principle stating that a person may not perform an act contrary to the public good.

puisne
Associate; subordinate; as distinguished from chief or superior.

punitive damages
See *damages, exemplary*.

purchase money
Money delivered by the buyer of real estate to the seller, without reference to whether the money might have been borrowed elsewhere and secured by a mortgage. The term relates to the *vendee-vendor* exchange and to no other.

136

purchase, words of
Words in a conveyence that refer to the person or persons to whom title is conveyed.

purport
To claim. The word carries a connotation of disbelief or falseness.

purview
Range; scope; extent.

Q B
Queen's Bench. See *King's Bench*.

qua *(Lat.)*
As; in the capacity of.

quaere *(Lat.)*
Query; doubt; question.

quantum meruit *(Lat.)*
As much as he merits. Where one party brings suit on an implied promise or an assumed contract.

quantum valebat *(Lat.)*
As much as it was worth. An action to recover the price of goods delivered on an implied promise to pay.

quare *(Lat.)*
Wherefore.

quare clausum fregit *(Lat.)*
Wherefore he broke the close. An action for trespass, to recover damages caused by unlawful entry.

quarter section
A quarter of a section of land; 160 acres.

quash
To make void; to overthrow; to annul; to supress.

quasi *(Lat.)*
Almost; as if; similar.

quasi contract
An implied contract; a contract arising from a relationship, without any express agreement between the parties.

query *(Lat.,* imperative *quaere)*
Question; to question or ask.

quia timet *(Lat.)*
Because he fears. A bill in equity to protect an interest one believes to be in jeopardy.

quid pro quo *(Lat.)*
Something for something else; in exchange for. Something exchanged.

quiescent
Dormant; inactive.

quiet
Undisturbed.

quiet title
A proceeding to remove a cloud from a title; to establish clear claim.

quitclaim
To relinquish all claims to property, or to acknowledge that one has no such claim.

quitclaim deed
A deed relinquishing any and all rights and interests that the grantor has, without identifying those rights or interests. Usually sought as protection against future disputes over title to property, when there is any question as to ownership.

quod vide *(Lat.)*
Which see. To refer the reader to something. Abbreviated q.v.

q.v. *(Lat.,* abbrev.*)*
Quod vide.

R *(abbrev.)*
Rex; Regina. King; Queen.

raise an issue
To bring up an issue in a pleading.

ratification
The authoritative adoption or confirmation of an action or a statute, by an individual, an official, or a legislative body.

ratio decidendi *(Lat.)*
The reason for a decision. The determining factor in a court's decision.

realty
Real estate; real property.

rebus sic stantibus *(Lat.)*
At this point of affairs. In international law, a doctrine that terminates an agreement because of changed circumstances, asserting that if the agreement is given continuing effect the results would not be those originally contemplated by the parties.

rebut
To answer; to defeat the effect.

rebutting evidence
Evidence introduced to disprove the evidence of an adversary.

recall
A procedure for the removal from office of a public official by a popular vote.

recall a judgment
To revoke or reverse a judgment, on the basis of fact.

receiver   See *receiver pendiente lite.*

receiver pendiente lite
An impartial person appointed by the court during litigation to oversee money and accounts, in the case of bankruptcy or foreclosure.

receivership
Being in the hands of a receiver.

recidivism
A tendency to relapse into criminal or antisocial behavior patterns.

recidivist
A habitual criminal.

reciprocity
Being reciprocal or mutual. Where jurisdictions, such as two states, exchange privileges or penalties for their citizens.

reckless
Careless.

recognizance
A type of bail bond, whereby a person will obligate himself to the court to appear in court at a later date to answer a charge.

recoupment
A defendant's right to hold back from damages to a plaintiff an amount equivalent to expenditures on a contract on which a plaintiff has brought suit, in cases where the plaintiff has not fulfilled his obligations under the contract.

recover
To regain; to win a lawsuit.

redemption
Repurchase; buying back. A right of redemption is an agreed-upon seller's right to repurchase an item sold from the buyer at an agreed-upon price.

redress   To receive reparation or indemnity.   **140**

redundancy
The introduction of extraneous and impertinent matter in a pleading.

referee
An officer duly appointed to hear arguments and arbitrate disputes and claims.

referendum
Plebiscite. The submission of a proposed law, or a proposed repeal of a law, to direct vote of the people.

referent
That which is referred to.

regnal
Referring to the reign of a sovereign.

rehearing
A second hearing on a matter already decided, for the purpose of presenting evidence previously omitted, for correcting errors, etc.

relation back (of amendments)
In an amended pleading, whenever a claim or a defense is asserted, and whenever such claim or defense arose from the same transaction as set forth in the original pleading, the amendment relates back to the original pleading as if it had been made at that time. See FRCP 15(c).

reliance interest
The interest of a person who has relied on the acts or words of another and has incurred loss for having done so. See Fuller and Perdue, The Reliance Interest in Contract Damages, 46 Yale Law Journal 52, 52-54 (1936).

reliction
An increase of the land by gradual or sudden withdrawal or retrocession of a river or sea.

remainder
An estate that is to take effect upon the termination of a prior

141

estate. A remainder may be *contingent*, if it is uncertain to take effect, or *vested*, if it is bound to take effect upon the happening of some necessary event.

remainderman
One entitled to a remainder.

remand
To return an action to a court from which it was appealed, for retrial or other reconsideration.

remedy
A remedial right to which an aggrieved party is entitled. The result of an action or the result for which an action is brought.

remittur
On appeal, the situation in which a new trial will be ordered unless the party for whom a decision was rendered agrees to accept a lesser amount than was awarded in the trial court, where a court of appeals believes an award to be too high. See *additur*.

remoteness
Where the connection between an injury complained of and a wrong done by the plaintiff is so tenuous that no compensation can be justly awarded.

removable claim
A claim that may be removed to another court.

removal of cause
Change of venue. Transfer of a lawsuit either from one state court to another, or from a state court to a federal court.

remuneration
Recompense; payment.

render
To give; to yield.

renvoi *(Fr.)*
Send back. In conflict of laws, the situation in which, when deciding a case under the *whole law* of a foreign jurisdiction, the forum may be faced with the problem that the foreign jurisdiction's choice-of-law rule would have the forum court decide the case by its own laws (renvoi). The forum court must then decide whether to accept the renvoi, or reject it, thereby determining whose *internal law* to apply.

repl. (abbrev.)
Replacement.

replevin
An action to recover possession of goods unlawfully taken and held by the defendant to the action.

replication
A plaintiff's response to a defendant's plea.

reprography
Copying by photographic or other process.

repudiate
To reject or renounce a responsibility or an obligation.

repugnant
Contrary; inconsistent.

requirements contract
A contract whereby a manufacturer or supplier agrees to furnish a purchaser with as much of a specified item as the purchaser may require for an established business.

res *(Lat.)*
Thing.

rescind
To cancel, terminate, or annul a contract, releasing the parties from all further obligation.

rescission of contract
An annulment or a repudiation of a contract

res gestae *(Lat.)*
The thing done. The acts and words of the participants in an event, which provide a clearer and more complete understanding of the event.

residuary
Having to do with a part remaining after other parts have been disposed of.

residuary legatee
See *legatee, residuary.*

residuum
A balance; a residue.

resile
To withdraw.

res integra *(Lat.)*
Whole thing. A point of law as yet undecided: i.e., one without precedent.

res inter alios acta, alteri nocere non debet *(Lat.)*
A transaction between other persons should not prejudice one not a party to it.

res ipsa loquitur *(Lat.)*
The thing speaks for itself. Where an incident itself presents an incontrovertible case of negligence, such as a surgical instrument remaining inside a patient following an operation.

res judicata *(Lat.)*
An adjudicated matter. A matter decided on its merits by a competent court. The judgment is conclusive unless reversed on appeal.

resolution
A decision of the court.

respondeat superior *(Lat.)*
Let the master answer. A principle that speaks to an

144

employer's responsibility for the negligent acts of his employees while they are working within the scope of their employment.

respondent
The party against whom a motion is filed; a defendant; an appellee.

restitution
Restoration of a right or property to one unjustly deprived of it.

restrictive covenant
A covenant restricting either land use or alienation.

retract
To take back.

rev. (abbrev.)
Revised; revision.

reversal
To revoke or reverse a judgment, on the basis of law.

reversible error
An error by a trial court that so affected the appellant's basic rights as to warrant a reversal of the decision below by the appellate court.

reversion
A residue of an estate in property, retained by the grantor or upon conveying an estate that is not whole. An alienable future interest retained by the grantor.

reversionary interest
An interest in a reversion.

revert
To go back to; to return to.

reverter
A reversion.

revoke
Cancel; rescind.

rider
In the preparation of legislation, a clause concerning an unrelated matter that is added to a bill after it has been through committee.

right
Right of action; an enforceable claim.

right-to-work laws
State laws that prohibit an employer from denying employment to a worker because of either membership or non-membership in a labor organization. Such laws outlaw closed shops and union shops.

riparian
Relating to or bordering the banks of a river.

riparian rights
Special rights accruing to owners of property bordering watercourses.

rogatory letters
A request by a court of one jurisdiction to a court of another jurisdiction, that a witness be examined by interrogatories accompanying the request. See 185 F. Supp. 832.

rule against perpetuities
No interest in property is good unless it must vest, if at all, not later than 21 years after some life in being at the time of creation of the interest. This rule nullifies ownership restrictions that prevent estates from vesting for an unreasonable period, or no longer than 21 years after the death of a specific person alive at the time the interest is created.

rule nisi
A rule or order that is bound to take effect unless the person against whom it is directed shows cause why it should not take effect. Also, *order to show cause*.

runaway shop
A plant that closes its doors and moves to a locale outside the area, to avoid the effects of unionization of its workers.

run with the land
A covenant is said to run with the land when its legal effect is passed with title to subsequent possessors of the land. As opposed to *in gross*.

S.A. (abbrev.)
Sociedad Anónima (*Sp.*); Société Anonyme (*Fr.*). Corporation.

Salic Law
See *Lex Salica*.

sanction
Power to enforce a law. Consent; condone.

satisfaction
Discharge or payment of a debt.

satisfaction piece
A written memo executed by a plaintiff and a defendant and filed with the court, acknowledging the satisfaction of a judgment. Also, a formal acknowledgment of payment of a mortgage.

SBA
Small Business Administration.

S.C.
Same case.

scab
A nonunion worker, especially one who works in the place of a union member who is out on strike.

scienter (Lat.)
Knowingly. A person's knowledge of the illegality of an action he performs. Knowledge of one's guilt. With regard to fraud, implies an intent to deceive.

sci. fa. *(Lat.,* abbrev.*)*
Scire facias (*q.v.*).

scintilla
Spark. The slightest bit or particle of evidence.

scire facias *(Lat.)*
Cause to know. A writ and a proceeding founded upon some record. The person against whom it is issued is to show cause why the record should or should not be suppressed. Abolished in federal actions. See FRCP 81(b).

Scrivener

scurrilous
Vulgar; using indecent language; foul-mouthed.

S.D.
Southern District. Refers to a state's district court.

seal
A wax impression. An impression made as an authenticating mark on a document, such as a corporate seal.

sealed verdict
A verdict arrived at when court is not in session, placed in an envelope and sealed, and read later in open court.

secure
To guarantee payment of a debt or obligation.

SEC
Securities and Exchange Commission.

secondary evidence
Evidence not from primary sources — e.g., a copy of a document or a reconstruction from memory.

section
In land measurement, 640 acres.

sedition
Insurrection; the promotion of acts of public disorder against the lawful government.

seisin
An interest in land, equivalent to legal ownership.

seize
To possess legally; to put in possession.

seizure
To take possession.

seller's lien
A right of a seller to retain all or part of goods sold until the buyer has paid the purchase price. Two preconditions of a seller's lien are that, (1) seller must have passed title to the goods to the buyer, and (2) those goods on which the lien is placed must be in possession of the seller.

seniority
An employee's length of time on a job or in a position, as compared with other employees of the same company. E.g., if A was hired on July 1, B on August 1, and C on September 1, A has seniority over B and C, and B has seniority over C.

sequester
To deposit; to set apart; to seclude, as to sequester a jury or witnesses during a trial.

sergeant at law
A member of a small and elite group of barristers in England who, until the Judicature Acts of the last century, had a monopoly on practicing in the Court of Common Pleas.

seriatim *(Lat.)*
One by one; in order.

service of process
The appropriate notification to a person that in some capacity he is concerned in a proceeding. Service may be in person or, in certain circumstances, by mail or by publication in a newspaper.

servient
Serving.

servient tenement
An estate in which another estate has an easement interest, which interest it is bound to respect.

servitude
Slavery; bondage.

set aside
To void; to annul irregular proceedings by declaring void a verdict or an award.

set-off
A counter claim or a cross-claim. A claim by a defendant, unrelated to but in response to a plaintiff's claim, wherein the defendant attempts to mitigate or extinguish the amount of the claim brought against him.

settlor
A person who creates an express trust by placing property in the possession of a trustee for the benefit of a beneficiary.

severable
Separable; for instance, one cause of action may be severable from another to which it was previously joined.

sham pleading
A pleading that appears good on its face but that is based on an error or errors in fact.

shepardize
In legal research, to consult *Shepard's Citations* of cases or statutes.

Shepard's
Shepard's Citations. A publication for use in legal research in which cases, references to cases and statutes, and other information are cited in convenient reference form.

shop steward
A person elected by members of a labor union to represent them in dealing with their employer and to enforce union rules.

shyster
An unscrupulous lawyer.

sic *(Lat.)*
Thus; so. Indicates that an error in a reproduced passage existed in the original and is not an error in the reproduction.

sic utere tuo ut alienum non laedas *(Lat.)*
Use your own [property] so as not to injure [that of] another.

simple contract
An oral contract or an unrecorded written contract that is not under seal.

simpliciter *(Lat.)*
Simply; naturally; summarily.

sine die *(Lat.)*
Without day. Signifying adjournment, without setting a day for another appearance.

sine prole *(Lat.)*
Without issue; childless.

sine qua non *(Lat.)*
Without which not. An indispensable element.

sit-down strike
A strike in which, once on the job, employees stop work and refuse to leave the employer's premises.

situs *(Lat.)*
Location.

slander
The malicious oral utterance of untrue defamatory remarks. Most forms of slander are not actionable, absent a show of actual damages.

SMSA
Standard Metropolitan Statistical Area.

solicitor
In English law, one who practices in the Court of Chancery.

solicitor general
An officer in the Department of Justice whose chief function is to represent the United States in actions to which it is a party before the Supreme Court or the Court of Claims.

s.p. (abbrev.)
Sine prole (*q.v.*).

spec. (abbrev.)
Special.

special appearance
See *appearance, special*.

special damages
See *damages, special*.

special judgment
A judgment *in rem*.

special master
A court-appointed official who is empowered to represent the court in a transaction to determine certain facts of the case and to ascertain the real circumstances.

specialty
An executed and delivered agreement or contract.

special verdict
See *verdict, special*.

specific performance
See *performance, specific*.

Speech and Debate Clause
Article I, Section 6, Clause 1, U.S. Constitution: "The senators and representatives shall . . . in all cases except treason, felony, and breach of the peace be privileged from arrest during their attendance at the session of their

respective Houses, and in going to and returning from the same; and for any speech or debate in either House, they shall not be questioned in any other place.

spendthrift trust
A trust created to provide maintenance through a trustee for one who would presumably squander the fund if it were accessible to him.

spite fence
A fence erected for the sole purpose of irritating a neighbor by affecting his access to air, light, or view.

spot zoning
Where one zoning status is applied to a certain property, while immediate surrounding properties have a different status. E.g., a single corner property in an otherwise wholly residential area may be zoned for a service station.

stakeholder
A disinterested party who holds funds that are disputed, either as a wager or for some other reason, with the understanding that he will turn the funds over to the successful party once the matter is settled.

standing to sue
Where a party has sufficient personal interest in obtaining relief, or where he is a sufficiently appropriate representative of other interested parties.

Star Chamber
A special court that during the reign of Henry VIII and afterward made arbitrary and unjust rulings, becoming synonymous with oppression. Also, *camera stellata*.

stare decisis *(Lat.)*
To stand by decisions. A flexible doctrine of the courts, concerning the force of precedent in deciding cases. Where a previous situation or set of facts gave rise to a decision, a similar situation or set of facts can be expected to give rise to the same ruling by another court.

stare decisis et non quieta movere *(Lat.)*
To stand by decisions and not to unsettle what is established.

state's evidence
Evidence produced by an accomplice to a crime, in testifying against his confederates.

statute of frauds
See *frauds, statute of*.

statute of limitations
A statute that fixes the amount of time during which an action may be brought, depending upon the type of action, the jurisdiction, and the circumstances of the case.

statutory
Created by or conforming to statute.

stay
To stop a proceeding temporarily by order of the court.

strict liability
Liability without reference to any fault, negligence, knowledge, or ignorance. Liability by association with an act resulting in harm to the person or property of another.

style
Name; title.

sua sponte *(Lat.)*
Voluntarily; on his own.

Subchapter S Corporation
A corporation that is permitted and elects to be taxed as a partnership, under Subchapter S of the Internal Revenue Code, thereby limiting individual shareholders' liabilities. Individual income is taxed, but the corporation is not taxed as a corporation.

subjacent support
The right of a property owner to have his land supported by the land, minerals, etc. beneath the surface.

sub judice *(Lat.)*
Before the court; for the court's consideration.

sub nomine *(Lat.)*
Under the name; in the name or title of. Indicating that the title of a case has been changed at some point in the proceedings. Abbreviated *sub nom*.

suborn
To bribe; to obtain another to commit perjury.

subpoena
A court order issued to command a person to appear to testify, under a threat of penalty in the event of failure to appear.

subpoena duces tecum
See *duces tecum, subpoena*.

subrogation
The substitution of one person for another, such as in the case of a creditor, thereby transferring the rights and obligations of the original holder to the person subrogated.

sub rosa
Secretly; privately.

subscribe
To write one's name at the end of a writing, such as a contract or will; to sign.

sub silentio *(Lat.)*
Silently.

substantial performance
In contract, where there has been performance on the substantial particulars, although not necessarily on less important details.

substantive law
The law that determines rights and duties, as distinguished from *adjective law*, which governs procedure or practice in legal matters.

substitute service
Service of process by legal means other than by personal service, whether by registered mail, by publication, or by some other acceptable procedure calculated to inform the person served.

sufficient
Adequate.

suffrage
The vote; voting.

sui generis *(Lat.)*
Of its own class; one of a kind.

sui juris *(Lat.)*
Of his own. Competent; not under any legal disability.

summary judgment
A judgment rendered on a motion by a party to a lawsuit, where pleadings, depositions, interrogatories, admissions, and other evidence show that there is no issue as to material fact, and that the movant is entitled to judgment as a matter of law. See FRCP 56.

summons
A notice to a defendant to appear at a specified time and place to answer charges being brought against him.

supersedeas bond
A bond obtained as surety for a suspension of judgment and a subsequent delay in execution on a matter pending appeal.

suppress
To prevent; disallow.

supra *(Lat.)*
Above; over.

Supremacy Clause
Article VI, Section 2, U.S. Constitution: "This Constitution

and the laws of the United States which shall be made in pursuance thereof; and all treaties made, or which shall be made, under the authority of the United States, shall be the supreme law of the land; and the Judges in every State shall be bound thereby, anything in the Constitution or laws of any State to the contrary notwithstanding."

surety
A guarantee; security.

surplussage
Something superfluous or unnecessary.

surrogate
Substitute; a judge in matters of *probate* and *intestate* succession.

surtax
A tax additional to a normal tax.

survive
To live longer than another.

survivorship, right of
Right to property of another upon having survived him.

suspect class
Any class of persons identified by a statute for special (discriminatory) treatment, in violation of Fourteenth Amendment equal protection guarantees, as construed by the court. E.g., classes identifiable by monetary worth, nationality, race, or sex.

sustain
To maintain; to uphold.

tacit
Inferred; implied.

tail
Reduced; curtailed, as a fee or an estate.

tail, fee
See *fee tail*.

tangible
That which has form and substance, and can be touched, as opposed to intangible.

tautology
Redundancy; needless repetition. E.g., "all by himself alone."

tax, ad valorem
A tax according to value; a percentage of the value of the taxed article.

tax, direct
See *direct tax*.

temp. (abbrev.)
Temporary.

tenancy in common
Where two or more persons hold an estate in a property, each having a right to occupy the property, with no right of survivorship.

tenancy, joint
Two or more persons, each holding an undivided interest in property, where that interest is created by a single instrument and with right of survivorship.

tenant
A person who holds real property.

tenant at will
A tenant who by the will of the lessor is allowed to remain in possession of a property, but whose right to remain may be terminated by the lessor at any time.

tender offer
An offer of payment in satisfaction of a debt or claim; an expression of a willingness to pay.

158

tenement
A holding or a right in property. See *dominant tenement* and *servient tenement*.

tergiversate
To employ evasions or subterfuge.

testament
A will. An instrument directing the disposition of a person's personal property upon his death.

testate
Having died leaving a will.

testator
One who has made a will.

testify
To give evidence under oath in court.

thing in action
See *chose in action*.

third party beneficiary
In contract, a person not a party to a contract, but who has an enforceable interest in it and for whose benefit the contract was made.

time is of the essence contract
A contract that emphasizes the importance of time limitations, and upon expiration of a stated time, neither party can demand an extension for performance.

timeliness
Happening at an opportune time.

title
Ownership. Certificate of ownership.

toll
To defeat; remove. To toll the statute of limitations is to show facts defeating its bar to an action.

tort
A civil wrong. A wrong done by one person to another and not arising from contract.

tortfeasor
One guilty of a tort. One who has committed a tort.

tortious
Wrongful.

to wit
To know; namely. Used to introduce lists.

toxicology
The science of poisons.

trademark
A mark or emblem affixed by a manufacturer to goods of his manufacture, to identify their origin.

transaction
A commercial art; interaction; contract. Any event giving rise to a cause of action; an affair.

transient
Passing through; transitory. Not permanent.

transitory action
An action on personal property; any personal action or one based on a transaction that might have occurred anywhere, as opposed to a local action.

transl. (abbrev.)
Translation; translator.

traverse
A denial of facts of a pleading. A traverse may be either general, denying all, or special, denying only certain allegations.

treasure trove
Found treasure.

160

trespass
An unlawful and harmful incursion on another's person or property, for which money damages may be awarded.

trespass on the case
At common law, a form of action for damages for an injury sustained by a party as an indirect result of a wrongful act of another.

trial per pais
Trial by jury.

trover
A form of action for the recovery of goods from a person who allegedly "found" them. A writ against wrongful detention of personal property.

trust
A fiduciary arrangement whereby one person holds title to and administers the property of another, to the benefit of the other.

trustee
One who executes or administers a trust.

turpitude
See *moral turpitude*.

uberrima fides *(Lat.)*
Utmost good faith.

ubi jus ibi remedium *(Lat.)*
There is no wrong without a remedy.

UCC
Uniform Commercial Code (q.v.).

UCCC
Uniform Consumer Credit Code (q.v.).

ultimate fact
A fact that is essential to the cause of action. A fact arrived at from evidence and reason.

ultra vires *(Lat.)*
Beyond powers. Applies to acts performed by a corporation that are beyond the scope of its corporate power, and to acts by a public body or official that are beyond the delegated authority.

UN
United Nations.

una voce *(Lat.)*
With one voice; unanimously.

unclean hands principle
One seeking relief in equity must have acted with probity and good faith in the transaction giving rise to his complaint. If not, he is not entitled to relief.

unconscionable
Unreasonable; unscrupulous.

unconscionable bargain
One that no man in his right mind would make and no honest man would accept.

underwrite
To insure.

Uniform Commercial Code
A code to regulate all aspects of commercial transactions, and accepted in all the states, with the exception of Louisiana. Abbreviated UCC.

Uniform Consumer Credit Code
A code that is being developed by the National Conference of Commissioners on Uniform State Laws and the ABA in an attempt to protect the consumer against unscrupulous business practices. Abbreviated UCCC.

unilateral
One-sided.

unilateral contract
A contract wherein only one side promises performance, receiving no promise of payment or performance in return.

union shop
A business or shop where new employees must become members of a union within a specified period of time.

United States Government Organization Manual
The official handbook of the United States Government. The *Manual* contains descriptions of the agencies of the legislative judicial, and executive branches, including brief descriptions of boards, commissions, and committees. It also contains brief statements of the quasi-official agencies and of selected international organizations. The *Manual* is published by the Office of the Federal Register, General Services Administration, and is available for $4.95 from the Superintendent of Documents, U.S. Government Printing Office, Washington, D.C. 20402.

unity of interest
In property, in the case of joint tenants all tenants must receive their interest by a single conveyance applicable to all.

unity of possession
In property, in the case of joint tenants all tenants have possession of the entire estate.

unity of time
In property, in the case of joint tenants all tenants must receive and hold their estate at the same time.

unity of title
In property, in the case of joint tenants all tenants must hold the same title.

unjust enrichment
Under the doctrine of unjust enrichment of the defendant, when a person holds goods, money, or property, either by misrepresentation, nondisclosure, or some other unfair practice, to his own enrichment and to the detriment of another, the latter may sue in equity to regain that which is rightfully his.

unlawful detainer
The situation that occurs when a tenant remains in possession of leased property after expiration of the lease term, or when he defaults in rent payments and neither pays nor moves out after the landlord serves him with notice to quit the premises.

unliquidated
Undetermined; not ascertained; unsettled.

usage of trade
Any practice or method of dealing having such regularity of observance in a place, vocation, or trade as to justify an expectation that it will be observed with respect to the transaction in question. UCC Sec. 1-205.

USC
United States Code.

USCA
United States Code Annotated.

USDA
United States Department of Agriculture.

usufruct
In the civil law, the right to use, enjoy, and make profits from property owned by another.

usury
Lending money at higher rates of interest than are allowed by law.

ux. (abbrev.)   *Uxor.*   **164**

uxor *(Lat.)*
Wife.

v. (abbrev.)
Versus; against. Also abbreviated *vs*.

VA
Veterans Administration.

vacate
To annul; to set aside, as a judgment. To move out.

valid
Good; of force.

validate
To make valid.

valuable consideration
Consideration of monetary value.

variance
In pleading, an inconsistency between allegations and their proof. In property, an exception obtained from authorities to allow for nonconformity with a zoning ordinance or a building regulation.

vel non *(Lat.)*
Or not.

vendee
A buyer.

vendor
A seller.

venire facias *(Lat.)*
Make to come. At common law, a writ to a sheriff to have him summon a jury.

venire facias de novo *(Lat.)*
Make to come again. A venire facias writ issued for a second trial, because of some irregularity in the first. Also, *venire de novo*.

venue
The county or other judicial district in which an action is tried and from which the jury is selected.

verdict
A jury decision concerning matters put before it.

verdict, special
A verdict finding the facts of a case, leaving to the court the question of the application of law to those facts.

vested
Established; fixed; not contingent upon some event.

vested interest
A vested right or interest in property, whether present or future.

vested remainder
See *remainder*.

vexatious
Harassing; annoying.

videlicet
See *viz*.

vi et armis
With force and arms. Direct force or violence.

vis à vis
Face to face; in comparison with; opposite to.

vis major *(Lat.)*
Force majeur (q.v.).

viva voce *(Lat.)*   With living voice. By word of mouth.

166

viz. (abbrev.)
For *videlicet*; to wit; namely. Used to introduce lists.

void
Without legal force; null.

voidable
That which can be made void.

voir dire
To tell the truth. A preliminary examination of a prospective juror or prospective jurors, to determine their interest in the case, qualifications, and competency.

volens *(Lat.)*
Willing.

volenti non fit injuria *(Lat.)*
To the consenting, no wrong is done. Where ordinarily an action for damages would lie, it may not if the person suffering the wrong has consented to the act that gave rise to the lawsuit.

voluble
Glib; talkative.

voluntary nonsuit
A nonsuit where a plaintiff abandons his case and allows the judgment and costs to go against him.

voting trust
An agreement entered into by shareholders in a corporation whereby their votes are cast in a block by a trustee. The object of the voting trust is to concentrate control of a corporation in a few shareholders.

voucher
A document that serves as evidence for a transaction.

vs. (abbrev.)
Versus; against. Also abbreviated *v*.

wager of law

In England, a type of trial in which a defense consisted of the defendant's swearing that the claim against him was unfounded and producing the requisite number (usually eleven) of compurgators, or oath helpers, to swear that they believed the defendant. The effect of the defense was a verdict for the defendant. Wager of Law was allowed only in cases of debt on simple contract and only on behalf of people of good character. Also called *compurgation*. Abolished in 1833.

waive

To abandon; to relinquish; to renounce.

waiver

Voluntary renunciation or surrender of a claim or right.

wanton

Grossly negligent; reckless; undisciplined; immoral.

ward

One in the care of a guardian.

warrant

Assure; promise. A writ issued by a competent authority for somebody's arrest.

warrant, bench

See *bench warrant*.

warranty of fitness

A statement of representation that goods are fit for the purposes for which they are sold.

watercourse

A stream.

W.D.

Western District. Refers to a state's district court.

weight of evidence

The preponderance of, or the greater evidence.

168

White Slave Traffic Act
See *Mann Act.*

whole law
In conflict of laws, the term which refers to the internal law of a state as well as to the state's laws regarding choice-of-laws.

wildcat strike
A strike by workers, without authorization of the union representing them.

will
An instrument directing the disposition of a person's real property upon his death. See *bequest, devise, testament.*

willfull, wilful
Intentional; voluntary.

windfall
Unexpected gain.

without prejudice
See *prejudice.*

without reserve
In an auction, reference to conditions of sale, that there are no prices reserved, or no minimum prices on the individual articles to be auctioned.

with prejudice
See *prejudice.*

words of limitation
See *limitation, words of.*

words of purchase
See *purchase, words of*

writ
A written order issued on the authority of the court.

writ of course
A writ that is granted as a matter of right, or to which an applicant is entitled as a matter of course, such as original writs and writs of execution. *Breve de cursu*. Writ of right.

writ of error
A writ issued by a superior court to a lower court to obtain a trial record for the purpose of reviewing the judgment and examining the record with regard to alleged errors in law.

writ of mandamus
A writ issued by a competent court to a public official, commanding him to perform some act that it is his duty to perform as an official.

writ of prohibition
A writ issued to a person directing him not to do something which the court is informed he is about to do.

wrongful death
Death caused by a wrongful action.

yellow dog contract
A contract in which an employer, as a condition of employment, prohibits an employee from joining, becoming, or remaining a member of any labor organization.

yellow journalism
The sensational and unscrupulous tactics used by certain newspapers in an effort to attract readers or to sway public opinion.

yield
Agricultural production. To surrender.

zoning
Local regulation governing the allocation of land resources for purposes of community planning.

zoning categories

Although precise definition of zoning classifications is a local issue, the following classifications may serve to illustrate a limited range of zoning possibilities:

R-A	Residential–Agriculture
R-1	Residential–low density
R-2	Residential–small lots
R-3	Residential–small lots
R-4	High-Rise Apartments
B-1	Neighborhood Business
B-2	Highway Business
B-3	Shopping Center
I-R	Restricted Industrial
P	Professional
O	Office

Municipalities and townships prepare zoning ordinance handbooks, which are usually available for a small sum at the Clerk's Office.